The Road to Second Degree Priesthood

The American Spiritual Alliance
Clergy Training Series
Book 2

The Road to Second Degree Priesthood

The American Spiritual Alliance
Clergy Training Series
Book 2

Rev. M. L. Rosenblad

MOON
BOOKS

Winchester, UK
Washington, USA

First published by Moon Books, 2014
Moon Books is an imprint of John Hunt Publishing Ltd., Laurel House, Station Approach,
Alresford, Hants, SO24 9JH, UK
office1@jhpbooks.net
www.johnhuntpublishing.com
www.moon-books.net

For distributor details and how to order please visit the 'Ordering' section on our website.

Text copyright: M. L. Rosenblad 2014

ISBN: 978 1 78279 647 3

All rights reserved. Except for brief quotations in critical articles or reviews, no part of this
book may be reproduced in any manner without prior written permission from the publishers.

The rights of M. L. Rosenblad as author have been asserted in accordance with the Copyright,
Designs and Patents Act 1988.

A CIP catalogue record for this book is available from the British Library.

Design: Stuart Davies
www.stuartdaviesart.com

Printed and bound by CPI Group (UK) Ltd, Croydon, CR0 4YY

We operate a distinctive and ethical publishing philosophy in all
areas of our business, from our global network of authors to
production and worldwide distribution.

CONTENTS

For my family and friends, but especially for my wife Chris and her unending patience and confidence in my work.

Phase 1: Principles of Applied Magick

Can you imagine what I would do if I could do all I can?
Sun Tzu

The application of Magick. In the realm of the stage magician, this is a simple task; distract the audience and then a rapid manipulation... voila! Not so when approaching true Magick. Ours is a far different arena. As you have already learned if you have read the first book in this series, drawing and focusing actual energy is the primary component in the application of all Magickal principles. Now we will begin to help you focus that ability on some of the things that can be achieved through its proper use.

By definition, Magick is utilizing intent, energy and focus to affect positive change in a specific thing. Positive change: let's consider this for a moment. Our ultimate goal is to do no harm; this makes it an imperative that we give considerable thought to our overall intent. All around us, we see those who advertise spells for love, revenge and many other things. Are these things of value? Revenge speaks clearly for itself, the opening intent is to do harm and this is not acceptable. Love – here is what many think is a grey area, but it is not so. It is acceptable to use Magick to help you find the right one for your life, but is doing harm if the tool is used to make that person fall in love with you. To do that is to bend their will and is doing harm. Many speak of the damage personal gain spells will cause. If the spell is used to create modest gain without doing damage, why would that be bad? It really would not. As long as greed is not the motivating factor, the Law of Power allows for it. As you can see, thought before action is vital to success, be mindful of Karmic return.

Entering your Higher Self is probably the most important aspect in the use of Magickal principles. Grounding and

Centering are practices which cannot be stressed enough; successful drawing of energy demands focus, a clear mind and well developed intent. Your ability to find, contain and focus energy is the key to its successful application. It is vital that everything you learned in your first steps in the Clergy becomes almost a daily practice. Magick is a tool and must be used safely; all the rules you have learned *always* apply.

Divination

By definition, divination is the act of seeking knowledge through the use of oracles, omens or so-called supernatural powers. This can be accomplished in any number of ways. In this section, we are going to briefly explore a number of the more common methods of divination. The goal here is to inform you of these methods and give brief descriptions, if you choose to pursue further knowledge you are free to do so. Remember that as Pagan Clergy; *divination is an integral part of who you are* and what you do. It is recommended that you find a form of divination that works for you and explore it more in depth. Find a mentor or a course on the discipline that feels most comfortable to you, but be careful in choosing because many courses are provided by charlatans only desiring to make money. All forms are useful, some, as will be explained, are a very physical part of many Rituals. One misconception of divination is that it reads the occurrence of future events and therefore is concrete. Nothing could be further from the truth, time is in a constant state of flux and individual action can and will alter future events, either for better or worse. Divination focuses more on the direction being traveled in the present, but a change based on that knowledge can and will alter future events.

The practitioner must always remember that in all things of a Magickal matter, you must only approach and act while working within your Higher Self. To neglect this will ultimately render your actions useless or, worse yet, damaging.

Tarot

Tarot is a form of divination that, contrary to popular belief, does not foretell the future; it brings to light that which is happening just under the surface. It allows us to look into our lives and gain understanding or confirmation of things we already knew but did not fully realize. The ideal in Tarot is to help the individual to make decisions and change course to avoid bad things or direct them on a course of good things that could potentially happen.

Carl Jung was the first psychoanalyst to attach importance to Tarot symbolism. He may have regarded the Tarot cards as representing *archetypes*: fundamental types of persons or situations embedded in the collective unconscious of all human beings. The theory of archetypes gives rise to several psychoanalytical uses. Since the cards represent these different archetypes within each individual, ideas of the subject's self-perception can be gained by asking them to select a card that they identify with. Equally, the subject can try to clarify the situation by imagining it in terms of the archetypal ideas associated with each card. For instance, someone rushing in heedlessly like the Knight of Swords, or blindly keeping the world at bay like the Rider-Waite-Smith Two of Swords. (**Wikipedia,** paraphrased from *Chaos and the Psychological Symbolism of Tarot* by Gerald Sheuler, Ph.D. 1997.)

The Tarot deck consists of 78 cards, 22 Major Arcana, which lead us through the passages of life's journeys and 56 Minor Arcana, which show the day-to-day occurrences.

There are four suits in the Tarot deck, these are:

Wands: Clubs
Cups: Hearts
Swords: Spades
Pentacles: Diamonds

As you can see, each of the four suits corresponds with our more common card suits. This is because at one time, it was a small crime to be caught with deck of cards (gambling), but a capitol crime to use them for so-called "witchcraft and fortune telling". The reader only carried the Major Arcana (these were the cards that, at the time, made it become witchcraft) on their person, thereby taking the greater risk, and relied on the person who was receiving the reading to supply the Minor Arcana (the Minor Arcana is what we today see as a simple deck of cards).

Each of the suits deals with a specific area of life and the suits further break into each of the four elements.

Wands / Fire: Work, enterprise, energies on the spiritual plane, the archetypical world.

Cups / Water: Desire, hopes, wishes, emotional activity, the state and forces of the mental plane and the creative world.

Swords / Air: Action, conflict of forces, the states and activities on the Astral Plane.

Pentacles / Earth: Things, possessions, concrete objects, the objectification of forces and energies of the higher worlds or planes represented by the prior three suits.

The cards are shuffled and then laid out in any one of a number of arrangements (these are determined by what type and how much information is desired). There are a couple of schools of thought surrounding the handling of the cards. Some readers insist that if you let anyone but yourself touch the deck it will destroy the psychic contact with the reader and the deck will have to be replaced or recharged. Others say that to achieve an accurate reading, the person seeking the reading must handle the cards or only the handler's energies will be read. Since historically the cards were never carried as a complete deck, one could reason that someone else handling the cards, at least in the case of the Minor Arcana, would have no detrimental effect. The choice would be up to the owner of the deck.

The use and arrangement of the cards is quite lengthy and could easily fill a book by itself. Also, the intuitive and interpretive skills required are somewhat extensive. In this lesson, it is the goal to give you a simple understanding of what the Tarot is and what it does. To become adept at its use requires time, practice and perseverance. If the Tarot is a form of divination that you would like to become proficient at, it is suggested that you carefully choose where your information comes from. Hundreds of books have been written on the subject, many of which were merely a way to make a profit and little else. To gain an accurate insight to the Tarot, *The Oracle of the Tarot: A Course on Tarot Divination* by Paul Foster Case is an excellent starting point. It can be found in the American Spiritual Alliance website library at **americanspiritualalliance.org** (available to registered students only).

Many things enter into the interpretation of the cards. As a reader, it is very important that you know and understand their intricacies. Here, we will give you a beginning, a foundation so to speak, for understanding. We will be using the Rider-Waite deck for our purposes because it is generally accepted as the most visually accurate of the great many available decks.

As we touched on lightly earlier, each suit has correspondences. These correspondences and values are very important to an accurate reading. Each suit also corresponds with the more common playing card deck of today, and may be used for readings, but with a loss of value because they would be missing the Major Arcana and the Page of each suit. Further, the frequency at which a suit appears in the layout of the cards has an impact in the reading.

The Minor Arcana is what would coincide with the modern playing deck and contains the Ace through to the King that most people are familiar with. It does have one card not found in today's playing cards, the Page. Each individual card of each suit carries a meaning and value which has two variations. Each card will have one meaning if dealt right side up and a separate and distinct meaning if inverted. While many today disregard the direction in which each card falls, failing to take this into account will result in a faulty or completely erroneous reading. I will refer you, once again, to *The Oracle of the Tarot: A Course on Tarot Divination* by Paul Foster Case. Two other extremely valuable books on this subject are: *Mastering the Tarot* and *The Tarot Revealed*. Both are by Eden Gray and are published by Signet Books.

Speaking Boards

Most know this form of divination as the Ouija Board. There has been a lot said, both positive and negative, about its use. Speaking Boards come in many shapes and sizes, they are commercially available, but buying and using one is not necessarily a good choice, especially for someone just learning the correct use of the Board (the reason will be explained a little later).

The most common version of a Speaking Board is the well-known Parker Brothers™ Ouija Board. Originally patented in the late 1800s, it became a favorite "game" of young people. Little or no thought was put into the potential consequences of the untrained using such a device.

Some say that the history of the Speaking Board goes back to Ancient Egypt, but there is not enough documentation to sustain the theory. They have been called Witch Boards, Talking Boards, and Ouija Boards, among other names. Much of this is based on the region in which you live or the Path you follow.

There are three components required in using the Speaking Board, the board itself, a planchet or a pendulum and the participants. The planchet is essentially a pointer with padded feet (to allow ease of movement on the board). The board must be smooth and without blemish, to allow the planchet to move freely over its surface.

A commercially made board is most often created from materials of an unknown source. In many cases, such as the well known Ouija Board, it is made from reclaimed materials from multiple locations which are ground up and then pressed into its final shape. Think about the problems of cleansing and purifying such a device. It could be riddled with negative energies from multiple sources and, as we have learned, some tools will reject purification.

As with most tools, if you can make it yourself, a part of your natural energies will be imparted to it, making it a part of you.

Prior to use, you should always purify the board and cast a Circle to ensure that you do not produce any negative or harmful energies or entities. Those who will be attending the board should also be cleansed of negative energy.

In practice, a small number of people (usually no more than four) would be seated at a small table (this is to allow each person to be able to place their fingertips very lightly on the planchet). The contact with the planchet is to place energy into it, making it a more usable tool for those called upon. One person asks a question and focuses on that question. If contact is made, the planchet will move freely around the board to the various letters spelling out an answer. If this is a true reading, there should be no manipulation by anyone seated at the board; it is fairly easy to tell if there is any misconduct if your fingers are relatively sensitive. Also, if this is done properly and you are given answers, there should be a sensation of energy (almost an electrical tingling) felt by everyone involved.

Scrying

Usually, when thinking of Scrying, most people see images of the TV series Charmed with the sisters holding a pendulum above a picture or a map. Although this can be done, it is not an accurate demonstration of what Scrying is or what it can do.

This particular form of divination, much like the Tarot, demonstrates what is occurring in the present time. The real difference is in the fact that it is much more visual, much like viewing a movie. During World War Two, the U.S. Government used a variation of Scrying, which it called "Remote Viewing". The people enlisted to this program successfully located a number of hidden weapons manufacturing and storage facilities. Law enforcement has also used it effectively in any number of missing persons and kidnapping cases.

Scrying is the use of an object (most of the time), usually a black mirror (preferably made of obsidian), a container of water or even a crystal ball. The object used can be almost anything because it is essentially simply a point of focus and visualization. It is the place you "see" the events in real time.

Some can develop their senses to a point that the use of an object is no longer necessary; the tool used is simply a focus point (a map or even a blank wall). At this point the practitioner is entering the Astral Plane. In this stage, the mind's eye will project the practitioner (Astral Self) to the location desired or needed. We will discuss the Astral Plane more completely later in your training. This particular level requires a very well developed empathy to accomplish it.

Scrying takes an intense amount of intent and focus to make it work properly; it is not a form of divination that comes easily or at all in some cases. It requires a high degree of empathic ability, which is not common in most people. It is also not always exact because it relies heavily on supplied information to direct the Seer to the needed information. If one piece of information is left out or inaccurate information included, it can redirect the images that are seen.

Runes

The Runes are among the most ancient known forms of divination. It stems from two forms of ancient Norse/Germanic alphabet, learning and divinatory tools and comes in more than one form, the Elder Futhark and the Younger Futhark. One of the oldest existing Rune Stones has been dated to roughly 100 BCE. The Elder Futhark is of Germanic dialect and contains twenty-four icons, each carrying both a letter of the alphabet and a specific sound. The Younger Futhark is Scandinavian in origin and contains sixteen icons.

When used in a divinatory manner, you will find that each individual Rune carries with it multiple and opposing values, much as is found in the Tarot.

There is, in more modern Rune sets, a blank Rune. This stone has been attributed to Odin (or often to the word Wyrd) and seems to be accepted in that meaning. However, it is widely published that in the 1980s a man by the name Ralph Blum (author of *The Book of Runes*), created that stone. He has been quoted to say he actually knew very little on the subject and sort of made things up as he went. This should make you think about sources when studying anything to do with the path as, even after his admission, this thought carries on. The Rune Ansuz is actually the stone most related to Odin. The term Wyrd is found in a number of Anglo-Saxon texts of the ancient era and has been defined to mean one's free will or fate.

The Runes work much as the more modern Tarot and require a deep empathic ability for them to work properly. The study of Rune divination is also much more involved than the more modern Tarot in that there are very intricate values placed on each stone.

Oracle

By definition, the previously discussed methods of divination are in fact all uses of oracles. For the purpose of this course, we will limit it to the direct communication with Deity or spirits, through a physical being.

Many of the metaphysical practices refer to this as

channeling. It is achieved by entering your Higher Self and then opening yourself (with specific intent) to the Astral Plane and allowing the needed entity to essentially speak through you.

Because of the fact that you are opening yourself in such a way, there is an inherent danger. This is not something to be taken lightly or attempted by someone without a great deal of experience. Historically, there are a number of rather famous oracles, the Oracle at Delphi being probably the most recognizable. There has been much speculation as to the validity of these ancient oracles and there are almost as many theories as there are scientists who have explored this arena.

In the more modern (and somewhat contested) practice of channeling, an individual who is highly empathic would open themselves to the Astral Plane and allow an entity to speak through them. This entity could be an ancestor or a member of one of the pantheons of Gods and Goddesses. They would be given the freedom to use the empath as a vessel to speak through. There are a number of individuals who became quite famous by channeling specific Deities and making a great deal of money in the process (whether they were in fact channeling or acting is not readily proven).

As with Speaking Boards, this practice can be somewhat dangerous because the empath is very open and if the area has not been properly protected and the Circle well cast, they can easily be influenced by negative and damaging entities.

Phase 2: Advanced Energy Work

Look deeper into nature and then you will understand everything.
Albert Einstein

Here, we will learn how to use the energies that have been spoken about so very frequently. Energy, both from within and without, is central to virtually all things we do. This is true of our day-to-day life and our life on the path.

Use of Minerals and Gem Stones

A First Degree student asked a very good question about this subject, regarding a similar use of gemstones to our path and uses in technology. I will start this chapter with an answer; in our Magickal practices, an energy source (internal energies for example) can be directed through a crystal or gem. The stone thereby amplifies and directs the energy for a specific purpose or intent. This same process is used in many ways in technology. From healing (the use of laser surgical techniques), to creating (plasma cutting tools), to destructive forces. Mankind's general use of crystals and gems requires an outside technological tool to harness these abilities. In Magickal workings, we utilize our inner self and allow it to combine with the inherent power within the stone to accomplish our intended goal.

In general, minerals, gemstones and crystals all contain and can help focus energy. Each object vibrates at a specific frequency and therefore carries within it specific types of energy. It is very important that you understand the properties of what you are working with; not doing so could interfere with your intent and render your task useless.

Once you have determined the correct stone, it is important that you form your intent and then enter your Higher Self. This will allow you to connect and align yourself with the corresponding frequency of the chosen material. This is accomplished through Grounding and Centering as well as placing yourself in a meditative state.

Once aligned with the object, it is a matter of focusing your intent through the material in an effort to narrow the band and direct it to accomplish your goal.

Creation and Manipulation of Energy

We spoke briefly about energy raising in your First Degree training. Here, we will go into a bit more detail on the subject. The creation of energy can be accomplished in any number of ways. One that is common on our path is the drum circle. If you have ever attended a drum circle, you would have found that as the tempo of the drums increased there was an almost electrical sensation associated with it. At a point of crescendo an abrupt halt to the drums causes an almost explosive sensation as the energy raised is released into the circle. Another well known method is chanting. In this technique, as in the drum circle, it starts slowly, building to a peak and stops. This creates two occurrences: one, it accomplishes the same thing as the drum circle and, two, it creates an alignment of frequency among those participating, further elevating the available energy. In both cases, most people who attune themselves to the activity are moved into a higher mental plane (Higher Self). This empowers any activity planned for inside the circle.

The Higher Self is a part of you that has always existed, but has become more or less dormant through the centuries. It is the part of you that is able to be in contact with the energies found in all things. Centuries of moral and peer pressure (which placed Magick in the realm of evil works), have forced man to stop using this portion of himself and now it is much more difficult to attain a state of oneness with the energy around us.

In practice, you do not truly create any other energy but that which is found within yourself. It is through elevating to your

Higher Self that you become aware of all of the energy that surrounds you. The Higher Self is capable of attuning to these energies and drawing them closer, this is accomplished by altering the frequency at which you vibrate to align with other energies. This allows them to be used as an instrument of positive change. The use of these energies is called manipulation, the drawing in of these energies and projecting them with intent and focus.

Focusing Created Energy

To properly focus created energy, one must have formulated intent prior to beginning to raising the available and needed energy. This act in itself requires great focus and presence of mind. Visualizing your intent while in your Higher Self will aid in focusing that energy in the correct direction. Your focus cannot waiver, a simple mundane thought allowed in will break the field you have created and thereby break the chain of events you are attempting to achieve.

Keep in mind both your receptive and projective hand; use them accordingly to draw upon that energy with your receptive hand, allowing it to flow through you into your projective hand. As the drawn energy flows through you, it will join with your physical energy. Many will use an external aid, such as a wand, in achieving this level of focus. From there, focus that energy toward your intent, be it a physical object or that of the non-physical. Speaking your intent while directing energy will also amplify and focus it. Again, utilizing a chant regarding your intent will empower your point of focus.

Phase 3: Beginning Spell Work

The universe is full of Magickal things patiently waiting for our wits to grow sharper.
Eden Phillpots

Here begins the art of spell writing. There are many do's and don'ts involved in the process. In spell writing, you must be ever mindful of our basic principles and guidelines as well as our ethical code. There are a number of Magickal subjects which would violate these things.

When preparing to design or use a spell, choose wisely, ask yourself, "Does this spell have any negativity associated with it?" A prime example might be love spells. While a spell to aid in finding your soul mate (that person you are meant to be with) would be considered positive in nature, one that is intended to cause a particular individual to fall in love with someone would be quite negative in nature. You may ask why this is; the answer is really very simple. A spell of this nature is designed to cause a person to do something he or she might never be inclined to do without Magickal intervention and this would be bending another's will. Since we are not supposed to impose our will on someone else, this act would be doing harm and considered very unethical. Never just jump to using a spell. If another avenue will do the same job, use it. We should not rely solely on Magick to fix or change things, Magick is a Divine gift and should not be used without thought, and it should be treated with the respect due a gift from Deity. Misuse will impact your ability to draw and create the energies needed in Magickal practice, the Divine granted us this gift, but she can also take it away.

Another thing to consider in this area, while receiving pay for Magickal services (readings and such) is acceptable, selling spells is not. The reason for this is, you may have created the spell for a specific purpose, but the buyer may have different designs for it. The buyer may have plans for that spell that go completely against the positive nature of what you created and that use would ultimately be your responsibility. Simply put, you have no control over how that spell is going to be used (unless you use it), but you will get the appropriate Karmic return for its use (you did, after all, create it). If you create the spell, it should be used by you and you alone, by doing that you will know the proper intent has been actually used. Selling the items to be used in a spell would have no negative Karmic return because there is no intent involved in the providing of materials.

Basic Spell Writing

As with all things of a Magickal nature, a spell must have intent, energy and focus to work. Even with all three of these things present, there is never a promise of success, so be prepared for that potential.

Many schools of thought exist as to what a spell requires to work (beyond focus, intent and energy). Some will say that it must be created in a rhyme structure; others will tell you that you only need to put your voice to your intent. I have found that either method is quite acceptable as long as your intent is included. What matters more than anything is that you are comfortable enough with it to put a positive attitude (intent) along with your spell. Writing a spell in rhyme is not always an easy proposition, but it does have the advantage of adding flourish. When we choose to add that flourish, you must ask yourself, "Am I doing this to add power, or simply to add showmanship?" If you are concerned with the value of what you are doing and not the wording that is what really matters. There is the fact that, in many cases, rhyme does add power and should be used, but not at the cost of inherent value.

A spell can best be described as a sort of prayer, you are sending a desire out to the Divine and hoping that she feels your intent has merit and therefore aids you.

Proper Timing for Successful Spell Use

The moon, sun, day of the week, even the time of day can have a profound impact on what you are attempting to accomplish. You, as a practitioner, should always plan these into the use of your spell.

Almost all those who write spells will consider the importance of the moon's phase, but rarely do you find them looking at the remaining things. All of the facets have impact; to ignore them will have influence on your intended action. Even if the moon is considered at a perfect point in phase for a specific spell, could the day of the week be in conflict with your desired intent? Or could solar influence possibly negate the value of your endeavor? All of this must be taken into account for any Magickal act to have the possibility of success.

Most are quite familiar with the power of the full moon, when it is in this phase you can do many things. It is considered by most to be the best time for charging and purifying Magickal tools and components. The new moon has traditionally been reserved for banishing spells or left alone completely because it might carry with it negative energy. These facts are so well passed along, that many do not understand the implications of timing beyond this point.

Rarely does anyone seem to concern themselves with the day of the week, time of day or solar positioning and effect when preparing for spellwork. Now this is odd, simply because when working on an astrological chart; one would consider all of these aspects or risk creating an erroneous chart. Would not the same implications have impact on any Magickal working? In truth, it does.

The days of the week have Magickal and elemental alignments just as everything else (a list of associations will follow). For example, it is a full moon and you wish to cast a protection spell.

The full moon just happens to fall on a Thursday. Could this have meaning to the value of your spell? In a word, YES. Thursday is associated with honor and loyalty and is a most effective day for spells of this nature. While it would not have a negative impact on your spell, it would diminish the outcome to a certain degree. In other words, your spell would not realize its full potential under these circumstances.

Sunday
Planetary Association: Sun
Color Association: Yellow and Gold
Gemstone Association: Quartz, Diamond, Amber, Carnelian
Herbal Association: Marigold, Sunflower
Deities: Brighid, Helios, Ra
General Associations: Agriculture, Beauty, Hope, Victory, Self-Expression, Creativity

Monday
Planetary Association: Moon
Color Association: Silver, White, Light Blue
Gemstone Association: Pearl, Opal, Moonstone
Herbal Association: Catnip, Comfrey, Sage, Chamomile, Mint (all types)
Deities: Thoth, Selene
General Associations: Childbearing, Family Life, Purity, Healing, Wisdom

Tuesday
Planetary Association: Mars
Color Association: Red, Orange
Gemstone Association: Garnet, Ruby
Herbal Associations: Thistle, Holly, Coneflower
Deities: Lilith, Mars, Ares, Morrighan
General Associations: War and Conflict, Marriage, Protection

Wednesday

Planetary Association: Mercury

Color Association: Purple

Gemstone Association: Aventurine, Agate

Herbal Association: Aspen Trees, Lilies, Lavender, Ferns

Deities: Odin, Hermes, Athena, Lugh

General Associations: Business and Job Related Issues, Communication, Traveling

Thursday

Planetary Associations: Jupiter

Color Associations: Royal Blues, Green

Gemstone Associations: Turquoise, Amethyst, Lapis Lazuli

Herbal Associations: Honeysuckle, Oak, Cinquefoil

Deities: Thor, Zeus, Jupiter, Juno

General Associations: Honor and Family Loyalty, Harvest, Clothing and Riches, Fealty

Friday

Planetary Associations: Venus

Color Associations: Pink, Aqua, Blue-Green

Gemstone Associations: Coral, Emerald, Rose Quartz

Herbal Associations: Strawberries, Apple Blossoms, Feverfew

Deities: Freya, Venus, Aphrodite

General Associations: Family Life and Fertility, Sexuality, Harmony, Friendship, Growth

Saturday

Planetary Associations: Saturn

Color Associations: Black, Dark Purple

Gemstone Associations: Apache Tear, Obsidian, Hematite

Herbal Associations: Thyme, Mullein, Cypress

Deities: Saturn, Hecate

General Associations: Agriculture, Creativity, Fortune and

Hope, Protection and Banishment of Negativity

Now we will discuss the lunar cycles and their importance to the timing of Magickal practice. Many teach that the best time for Magickal workings is at midnight on a full moon. While this does work, it is not entirely accurate as you will see. There are nine total phases in a lunar cycle. There is a modern school of thought that does not consider five of them as actual phases, but they have been used for centuries effectively, and there are some who teach that there are only four phases but this leaves out a great deal of Magickal influence. Each has specific powers and energy and can impart much more strength into your work if taken into consideration.

A *waxing moon* (during the seven days after a new moon) is the best time for working in the areas of love, growth, courage, elemental Magick, luck and friends. As a general rule, this can be best achieved around sunset (more precise timing can be used and we will cover that shortly).

The *waning moon* (during the seven days after a full moon), is most valuable for works dealing with protection, banishing disease and illness, stress and addictions (regardless of type). The rule of thumb is to do these works between midnight and noon.

During the *full moon* psychic energy is at its most powerful, making this a time for prophecy and divination. The full moon occurs fourteen days after the new moon and is best suited for dealing with health and fitness, decisions, dreams, family, protection, motivation and wisdom. While doing Magickal work under a full moon, midnight is often cited as the best time; and as a general rule, this does work, but there are ways to make the energies work much more in your favor as you will learn.

The *new moon* has a very specific time line for use in Magickal practice, from the peak of the first day of this phase to three and one half days after. Use of this moon phase is generally performed between dawn and sunset. It is best suited for self improvement, romance, protection and agricultural aspects.

A *gibbous moon* is from ten to thirteen days after a new moon and is a good time for works involving patience, purity, centering emotions and courage. This has a very short working timeline which is usually set between 10pm and 11pm.

The *disseminating moon* falls between three and seven days after the full moon at around 3am and is known as the time of souls. This is one of the shortest in duration for Magickal workings and is best suited to communication, calming, knowledge and decisions.

The *dark moon* is from eleven to fourteen days after the full moon and is most powerful during the day at around 10am. This time is best suited for dealing with obstacles in life.

A *void moon* occurs multiple times during each month (or complete lunar cycle). As the moon ventures out of each phase (roughly every two and one half days), it is considered *void*. Of course, this means that Magickal energies are unreachable (it is sort of a mini vacation for the moon). During these days, you are best to meditate, ground and center, but do not bother performing any Magickal workings, because there will likely be no response.

To further complicate timing, the moon during each phase has a peak or time of greatest energy. This does not always occur at the same time of day during each cycle because of the path the moon follows through the sky. Since man began using agriculture, he found that certain times (meaning exactly that, time of day) had different effects on how crops grew. Healers found that these same things influenced their practice. Hunter-gatherers found greater success at specific times of day or night. The energies of the moon do not always peak when the moon is at its most visible (at night), it can occur at any time during a given twenty-four hour period. There is a very detailed mathematical process that will give you this precise time, but, unless you are an astronomer with the proper equipment, I suggest that you simply purchase a *Farmer's Almanac*. These times are so important that they are listed by precise time in almost every almanac available; many list the exact times for the peak of each phase as well as when the moon is in void. Not using precise times will not negatively impact your workings, but by using them, you will increase the energies related to what you are doing and create a stronger likelihood of success. When combined with the correct associated day, you increase the energies even more.

Our sun has immense power and its cycles work in a very different way than those of the moon. Unlike the moon, the sun crests its peak of power and influence once a day instead of once a month. Its four daily phases also align with the four seasons. Sunrise would best be described as the equivalent of a waxing moon. It is aligned with the Spring Equinox, the mid-day would be quite similar to the full moon in power and is associated with the Summer Solstice. Sunset is the waning phase of the sun and is associated with the Autumnal Equinox. Midnight (when the sun is no longer visible and darkness surrounds us) would be similar to the dark of the moon and is aligned with the Winter Solstice.

As you can see, Magickal practice is not simply writing and casting spells, great thought and planning must enter into every-thing you do if you wish to achieve the greatest potential for success. Intent, energy and focus are necessary in our works and to create ample energy, all things must be considered. You can easily place your focus on individual patterns of the days, the moon or the sun and have great success in your workings or you may choose to factor all into what you are trying to accomplish; just be mindful that each area has power and in proper combi-nation great things may be accomplished.

Phase 4: Group Leadership Responsibilities

Management is doing things right; Leadership is doing the right things.
Peter Drucker

With leadership comes great responsibility. You will encounter many rough roads during the course of your path and few, as a member of the Clergy, will be easy. You will be placed in positions of decision that will regularly tax your faith and spirituality. It is your duty to always demonstrate through your words and actions a devotion to Deity while still being able to make the correct decisions. The choices you make are a direct reflection on you as a leader, but carry the additional weight of how your group, path and tradition are viewed by those who are in contact with you.

Leadership

To be an effective leader requires positive intent, great focus (there are those words again) and a willingness to listen to those you lead.

As a member of the Clergy, you are bound by your spiritual path and your dedication to the members of your group. You must, in your day-to-day life, place these things as paramount. To do less would be a disservice to your calling.

Maintaining a group, be that group a small circle, a coven, grove, shrine or even a standing temple or church requires that you, as the leader, look to the needs of everyone within that group and create an environment that will promote the positive, spiritual needs of that membership. You must also realize that it will be virtually impossible to make each and every member happy all of the time. You will have a heavy burden when it comes to making choices and taking action. A strong leader not only understands the value of saying no, but also the need to look to alternative ideas that will both maintain the value of your group while not stepping away from your responsibilities and the principles of ethics of your group and tradition.

First and foremost is your duty the Divine, keeping this in mind, you need to act accordingly to help foster that thought in those you lead. Your stance, in regard to principles and ethics, must be strong; but handled with compassion and under-standing. The strongest and most effective leaders do not demonstrate an "iron fist", controlling everything around them; they assess every situation and take the most reasonable and beneficial course of action. They take the time to communicate with their members and learn about their views, ideas and hopes. In doing this, you can work more directly with potential issues, improve your group and help it grow and flourish.

Dealing with Antagonists within your Group

As a leader, you will discover that on occasion, there will be antagonists within your group. These individuals can be quite subtle in their approach. Often they will work closely with you, offering to lend a hand and in the beginning, presenting you with a great deal of valuable effort. I am not saying that every person offering to help will be antagonistic; however, it is very important that you learn to recognize the signs. Many a group has been destroyed from within by not recognizing a problem and dealing with it accordingly.

An antagonist is an individual who creates dissention within the organization, one who ultimately cannot be happy with the group or its members and becomes destructive in the process. They will usually act in a couple of ways. Antagonists might spread rumors within the group, about another member or even the leadership themselves, which have no basis in fact. Another method is posting those same rumors on social websites. Sadly, we live in a world where these things can easily take root and grow. When they start to grow, great damage can be done if not handled properly.

You have been taught to harm no one, but remember, you have also been taught to protect those things of importance. You have a number of actions available to you, some are good and some will guide you to total failure, here we will talk about the do's and don'ts when dealing with antagonistic behavior.

The first action most feel is appropriate is defensive rage, which promotes confrontation. This is almost always counterproductive to you and your group. Acting out in anger usually sends the message that the rumors and allegations are true. "If they are that angry, do they have something to hide?" This is most often the first thought of those seeing an angry response. Pause, take a moment, think about the issue; ask yourself, is there any basis in fact? Could someone perceive anything I or we have done to be an issue? Do not allow yourself or your group to enter into a standing battle that will ultimately make both parties look bad. Remember, it is your duty to maintain the standing of your group, not damage it.

In most cases, antagonists are people who by their very nature need to create conflict and issues in an effort to create self worth and importance. If you as a leader choose to confront them directly, it often gives them the resource of becoming the victim of attack by you. This can allow the situation to become a far larger issue than it was in the beginning. Often, when confronted directly, the antagonist will take no responsibility for any of their actions. The more appropriate response is to not acknowledge or respond to them and do not bring the subject up with anyone unless you are directly asked (by someone other than the antagonist). This will accomplish, through a passive means, that this individual's accusations have no basis.

One tool that I often use in dealing with antagonists is our organization's code of conduct, which is a document that every member must read and agree to by signing off on it. I am including it here simply to give those who are not members of our organization a potential tool of defense. Our affiliate groups use this in their organizational documents and you are free to use it in its entirety or as a template for your group. I would ask that if you choose to use this that you remove the reference to our organization and realize that you are utilizing this document without encumbrance (legally or otherwise).

Code of Conduct

We the founding Members, Charter Members, General Membership and Affiliates, in an effort to create an improved relationship and environment of understanding with the so-called "Mainstream" world at large, hereby acknowledge, adopt and subscribe to the following Code of Conduct.

Section one: "Harm None"

1) Realizing that all life is sacred to the Divine and in keeping with the "Harm None" philosophy of our path, we as an organization choose to refrain from doing physical damage or to take life wantonly. Our belief forbids us from harming our fellow man except in defense of ourselves or others and also forbids the taking of animal life for any purpose other than providing us with sustenance. We choose to take no animal's life for the purpose of extermination or as merely a "trophy". We will avoid any physical confrontation with other people and will always strive for a peaceable resolution.

2) Understanding that every individual has the inalienable right to their opinion, we will not infringe upon that right with a singular exception. No member of this organization shall make any public statement or subscription to a political philosophy while acting in the capacity of this institution or its affiliates. This does not preclude any

member from acting as an individual at any other time.

3) As both an "Earth-Based" and Interfaith organization, our members are expected to refrain from making any statements that can be considered inflammatory, derogatory or insulting to or about any other Religious path. This includes public statements and postings on social media venues. Our ultimate goal is to improve the existing environment between any and all faiths and such acts would be detrimental to this resolve.

Section Two: Ethics

1) Every person has the right to free will and choice and this organization cannot and will not infringe on that right, however, when attending a public venue and acting in our capacity as members; it is incumbent on each member to present themselves in the most positive light possible. Courtesy is paramount. This includes actions, choice of appropriate attire and statements.

2) If, while attending an event, the host asks for your assistance; it is expected that (when possible) our members be willing to help as long as this assistance does not infringe on the members or our organization's ethical beliefs.

3) Each member should strive to leave a good impression of themselves and the organization (if representing themselves as members) when attending a public event of any kind.

4) Respecting other's personal property is expected at all times.

5) Each member shall respect local, State and Federal laws at all times.

This provides an "out" so to speak because to violate these concepts allows the leadership of the group to simply remove the offensive party. By doing this you remove their power. If you choose this recourse, do not make any public commentary about the subject, but document the action you have decided to take and maintain that documentation.

Media and Public Contact

This is the area with the most potential issues because it is here that you will have to face the many myths and misconceptions of your belief. Your actions and words will be either your greatest ally or your worst enemy.

Media and public contact go hand in hand. Any public event has the potential for media coverage; so be prepared. Your actions and words, as have so often been pointed out, can place you and your organization in either a positive or negative position. A simple comment overheard or misinterpreted can devastate your standing. It is your duty as a member of the Clergy to always demonstrate compassion and understanding, to do less will open the doors to any manner of damaging issues.

You may be approached by a member of the media for a comment or possibly an interview, if you are not prepared; allow yourself the privilege of making no comment, or arranging for an interview at a later time. There is no harm in allowing yourself time to prepare. If questions go beyond the scope of your expertise, direct them to contact someone in a higher leadership position in your tradition (but let the leader know you have done this, no one likes to be caught off guard). If you are not able to do that and feel you must respond, think clearly before answering and if a question seems leading, always ask for clarification. If a question seems demeaning or based on myth, take a moment to choose how you answer. This might be a door that can lead to better understanding; should you answer in a way that deflates the myth or insult.

Public events can serve to inform and enlighten those outside the path to the many positive aspects of our faith, but always keep in mind that we are not here to convert, but rather to educate. If someone shows interest in learning more, by all means answer their questions, but in doing so, always choose your responses wisely. Use caution and do not try to answer for all paths, preface your answer with a response that demonstrates what your tradition or path believes because each path has a different stance on many subjects. If you know your tradition's principles (as you should), stay within the confines of them and you should not be misinterpreted.

Fiscal Responsibilities

Money and how it is handled has caused more issues to groups than any other area. It is vital to maintain a system of "checks and balances" for a number of reasons. Whether you are a 501(C)(3) or a Constitutional Free Church, your financial records are a matter of public availability and are always subject to audit. This is so that it can be determined how your organization uses its funds. There are very strict lines on how money may be used by a religious organization and to fall outside of these lines can be cause for removal of your Tax Exempt status. One of the most well known areas is the legal separation of Church and State. For a religious organization to support, endorse, provide money or accept money from a political source is a very dangerous area and often leads to loss of exempt status. Never walk in this area.

While the vast majority of religious groups do not bring in enough money to warrant having an accountant on staff, an effective ledger or bookkeeping software and someone who knows how to use it (your treasurer) is vital, not optional. These records must always be kept up to date and receipts maintained as they can be called upon at any time for review. It is also a wise choice to provide quarterly reports to your leadership, if you are a 501(C)(3), it is not an option.

Always keep in mind that just because you are the leader of the group, you do not have the right to just make purchases. The organization's money is not yours and must be used by and for the organization. You should always obtain agreement from your leadership council prior to making any purchases. By doing this, you will eliminate any questions of motive or corruption before they can take root.

A simple rule of thumb, maintain all receipts (all financial documents for that matter) for a minimum of seven years. Create a filing system for them and do not lose or misplace any of these receipts or documents, the ones that "disappear" are the ones that will haunt you.

Phase 5: World Religion: An Introduction to Religious Philosophy

Faith is believing in things when common sense tells you not to.
George Seaton

As a member of the Clergy, it is your responsibility to have an understanding of the many belief systems found in the world today. There are a great many similarities to be found amongst all beliefs. There are also many differences. It is important, to be a successful leader, that you have a degree of knowledge of these things. This will help you answer questions from your members, allow you to communicate successfully with members of other beliefs and assist in matters of public need.

Understanding Many Religions

Why is there is a need to learn about and understand different belief systems? This is a question that has been asked many times over countless years. In times past, distance minimized that need. In our modern, more compressed, world it has become a vital part of any belief system's very existence. We live in a society that places us in direct contact with so many varied ideologies that without understanding, we cannot function in accord. Lack of knowledge only serves to further the many misconceptions and bigotry found in so many communities.

By working to understand, we create an environment of acceptance and the ability to move forward. The tool of under-standing is the one tool which aids in the creation of bridges, the embodiment of a bridge leads to cooperation and brotherhood. These two things lead to breaking down the barriers of religious bigotry and misconception.

How Does it Benefit a Temple or Church?

By striving for understanding, your group will only flourish; it builds a bridge of trust. This in turn creates an atmosphere of acceptance, fellowship and cooperation; all things we want to attain so that we may work more closely with our fellow man. It allows us to answer accurately the many questions that, as a Clergy member, you will hear. As that acceptance and cooperation grows, so does trust and understanding; which in turn dispels many of the myths and misconceptions of our path which have been created over a number of centuries.

Concepts, Tenets and Ideals

Similarities and Differences among Religions

Virtually all beliefs systems, at their core, have very similar value systems or ideologies. Some of these include the concept of free will, a "golden rule", honesty, a personal relationship with Deity. Here, we will look at the historical aspects of a few of the religious beliefs, their founder's ideology and how these have changed or remained the same through the generations.

The causative factor in many of the similarities found in each religious belief can, in many cases, be traced directly to doctrine found in the "mother" religion which would be used either in its entirety or with minor modifications by the founder of the new religion. In cases of similarity between religious cultures that at the time of their founding had no means of contact with beliefs also using specific tenets, a great amount of theory and conjecture occurs. One theory involves the idea that a singular entity or Deity visited these many cultures and imparted a philosophy that, while continuing to present the same message, did so in a way that was more readily assimilated by these different cultures.

You will have the opportunity to learn how many belief systems have evolved since their creation. In a world filled with religious bigotry based on centuries of misinformation, this section will serve you well. While we will not dwell on the negative, we will show how, through the evolution of a belief, certain negative aspects have come into play and how they affect a belief overall.

A Brief Comparative History Lesson

We will focus here on three religious philosophies in an effort to demonstrate the numerous ways they differ and yet follow a similar pattern. Each of these philosophies is actually an umbrella that various denominations of belief fall under; they are the Abrahamic belief, Eastern belief and Paganism. These "titles" are used because they have become the accepted method of classifying religious groups. There are far too many beliefs and denominations within each to easily catalog, so categorizing became a necessity. Here, we will cover but a few of the more well known beliefs and provide you with a brief history, structure and some comparisons to earlier belief systems.

Most beliefs have a central motivating character or founder. This may not be quite as apparent in the umbrella of Paganism because, prior to 1951, most teaching was handed down verbally and little was recorded in writing for the future, but can be found within a number of the denominations or sects found within it. I would like to note here that because of the historical method of verbal education, many things that have been taught in modern Pagan culture are based on the understanding and opinion of each group's creators.

We will begin with a comparison of the Abrahamic faiths; these include Judaism, Islam and Christianity. The name given to this umbrella is based on the covenant "God" made with the prophet Abraham (roughly translates to "Father of many nations"). An interesting note; Abraham had his first son with his Egyptian handmaiden Hagar at the insistence of his wife Sarah because they had no children. This son was named Ishmael, who later became the focal individual in the creation of Islam and has been deemed by that belief as the perfect Muslim. Abraham's second son (conceived with Sarah) was named Isaac. He is considered the beginning of the seven tribes of Israel. Hagar and Ishmael were driven out into the desert by Abraham at Sarah's request shortly after the birth of Isaac.

Judaism

Of the Abrahamic faiths, Judaism is considered by far the oldest. Credited as being founded in about 1300 BCE by Moses in what is now known as Palestine, this timeframe is somewhat disputed by some schools of thought, but is the most common estimation of date. Its early growth stages were primarily confined to Palestine, with little to no growth in outlying regions. Moses is known as the author of the Torah and is the central most important figure in the Jewish culture. It is written in the Bible that Moses was born to a slave family in Egypt, but was placed in a basket and floated on the river to save him from the decree of Pharaoh that all newborn male children of the slaves be put to death. He was found, adopted and raised in Pharaoh's royal household, destined to be a Prince of Egypt. His name was defined in the Bible as Moseh (the one who was drawn out).

Moses ultimately rejected his upbringing, which fulfilled the prophesy leading to his being placed in the basket in infancy, and led the enslaved people out of Egypt where they wandered in the desert for about forty years (as described in the Bible). They stopped at Mount Sinai where Moses went up the mountain and remained for a time, although we will not go into scriptural detail about his stay there. Upon his return to the people, he presented them with two tablets containing the Ten Commandments (ostensibly written by the hand of God). These Ten Commandments, which were placed in the fabled Ark of the Covenant, became what is now referred to as Mosaic Law and was adhered to by his followers; this could be considered the birth of the Judaic faith. A note of comparison; the Ten Commandments are found in a much older document that is closely associated with Moses' upbringing and education as an Egyptian Prince. This document is the Papyrus of Ani (part of the Egyptian Book of the Dead) and it contains the 42 negative confessions, the tablets that Moses provided to his people as law would seem to have been generated from his original religious education. It is estimated that the scrolls are in the realm of 3,200 years old, which would pre-dated Judaic culture by a number of centuries. Ancient Egyptian religion, due to its polytheistic (many Gods) structure, would fall into the Pagan family.

In our modern time, Judaism ranks as roughly the twelfth largest religion worldwide and follows most if not all of the original tenets as prescribed by Mosaic Law. Followers still subscribe to the Torah, which is also used by modern Christians as the Old Testament and contains the five books of Moses: Genesis, Exodus, Leviticus, Numbers and Deuteronomy. There is the oral Torah (which is said to have been taught to Moses by God) and the written Torah (Tanakh). The Tanakh contains the Torah (the Law), the Nevi'im (the Prophets), the Ketuvim (the Writings) and the Holy Scriptures. The Judaic culture views Jesus as a false prophet and does not acknowledge him in any way. The New Testament of the Bible, which is primarily the testament of Jesus, is not of Judaic creation and is not considered to be the word of God. They also view Islamic faith as a false extension of Judaism. The culture forbids the use of statues for iconic representation because it feels that this is a form of idolatry and therefore an abomination to God.

In Judaism's beginnings, a man having multiple wives was rather commonplace and not considered an adulterous act. However, this concept has been rejected over the centuries and is now considered objectionable.

The Clergy structure within the Judaic faiths are:

- The Rabbi, who is the duly ordained leader and primary teacher in a Synagogue;
- The Cantor, who is responsible for the liturgical portion of Temple and sings chants or prayers;
- The Scribe, who is versed in the nature of Judaic law and whose job it is to transcribe and interpret the Torah; and
- The Mohel; this is the man who performs the Brit-Milah or ritual circumcision in accordance with Abraham's original Covenant with God.

The culture is strictly monotheistic, believing in a singular God (known as HaShem which means "the Name" or Adonai which translates to "the Lord") in a singular state. There are specific sects of Judaic faith that do, in fact, believe in reincarnation (a common belief among those under the Pagan and Eastern umbrellas), but they are quite rare.

Christianity

Christianity was ostensibly founded by Jesus of Nazareth in 32 CE-33 CE. There are scholars who say the actual founding of the faith began after his crucifixion in approximately 33 CE, and was done by his disciples. For many years there was controversy as to his existence, but most scholars and historians now agree that he did exist, although to what extent is still an issue with some. This is not to say that he was, in fact, the Messiah as he was called, but that his life does hold historical significance.

Jesus was born into a Jewish family; he is said to have been conceived by a virgin woman (Mary) by the hand of God. Little is told of his youth except that he "taught" in the Temple at age twelve. Beyond this point, his story is quite cryptic until he is about thirty years old. At this stage in his life he is found teaching a concept of the "Kingdom of God" and a move away from the Judaic faith. He had twelve primary followers who were essentially with him continuously during his adult years.

35

It is said that he performed many miracles ranging from healing the sick to raising the dead during his last years on Earth. Most say that this is the proof that he was truly the Son of God.

While he taught his philosophy, the Sanhedrin (the primary Jewish judicial group) prepared what many have considered an illegal trial based on his heretical teachings. In his trial, he was beaten and ridiculed for his claim of being the Son of God. One should note that in Isaiah 44:6 it states: "I am the first, I am the last and beside me there is no other God." This was interpreted by the Sanhedrin as, God had no Son. The Jerusalem Talmud explicitly states: "If a man claims to be God, he is a liar." (Ta'anit 2:1) Another example of this would be found in the Mishneh Torah (*Hilkhot Melakhim* 11:10–12).

Jesus is said to have prophesied his death at a meeting that has become known as the last supper. During this supper, Jesus said that one of those present (a disciple) would betray him. He also performed something of a ritual with bread and wine:

And he took bread, and when he had given thanks, he broke it, and gave to them, saying, "This is my body which is given for you: this do in remembrance of me." And the cup in like manner after supper, saying, "This cup is the new covenant in my blood, [even] that which is poured out for you." (Luke 19-20)

Although a symbolic gesture, this act is similar to that of a practice found in the Egyptian Papyrus of Ani which says (paraphrased) that to eat the flesh and drink the blood of someone will grant you their traits and characteristics.

After his conviction by the Sanhedrin, Jesus was taken before Pontius Pilate, since they were not able to sentence him for any crimes. He was asked to judge and condemn him. In Luke 23:14-16 Pilate stated publicly that he saw no fault in Jesus and nothing worthy of execution, but the Elders convinced him to pass on a sentence of crucifixion.

His teachings were carried on by his twelve disciples and his word was spread widely around neighboring nations, causing it to grow far beyond Palestine. It has continued to grow and flourish throughout the world over the centuries (with many modifications and new denominations growing from these modifications) making it the largest religious belief system in the modern world.

Modern Christianity views Judaism as a true religion, but also as an incomplete religion because of its followers' denial of Jesus of Nazareth's divinity. They also view Islam as a false religion because it denies his divinity, while showing respect for him as a prophet.

This belief system is Trinitarian/Monotheistic, which means it sees God as a singular entity with three separate aspects. These would be God as the Father, God as the Son (Jesus) and God as the Holy Spirit. This Trinitarian aspect can be found in a number of the early Pagan philosophies, Maiden, Mother, Crone (Wiccan) and the Three Fates (Clotho, Lachesis and Atropos) in Greek Paganism to name but two.

The leadership structure is found to vary based on denomination but, for the most part, is built of:

- The Minister or Priest, an ordained member of Clergy who is responsible for the religious education of his/her parish or church;
- Church Elders, who are responsible for the operation of the church and participate in religious services; and
- Lay Ministers, who are individuals who have in-depth knowledge of their faith and who work in the community to bring new members into their Church.

Islam

The Islamic belief was founded in about 622 CE by the Prophet

Muhammad when, it is said, God chose him to teach his countrymen there was only one true God. This message was given while he was meditating in a cave on Mount Hira by the angel Gabriel. The message was to recite, "In the name of thy Lord who created, created man from a clot of blood." (Quran 96:1-2) This command was repeated three times as Muhammad denied his ability to do it. He finally recited what were to become the first five verses of the 96th chapter of the Quran.

He had many revelations which ultimately were placed into writing; this writing became the Holy Book of the Islamic faith, the Quran. He spread the word that the oneness of God was paramount and from this all things followed. His message was initially rejected by many, but this only served to strengthen his resolve. This rejection became persecution and after about ten years of growth, Muhammad sent a group of his followers to Ethiopia (which was a Christian governed location). The Christian ruler extended his protection to them (this has been cherished by Muslims ever since). With a sentence of death over his head, Muhammad set out to Yathrib in an effort to build his movement. This city was eventually renamed Medina ("The City").

The Constitution of Medina afforded (with a nominal tax and adherence to Islamic law) freedom of religious pursuit for Christians and Jews, but expressly forbade any polytheistic practices.

The Quran says, "Verily the most honorable of you with God are the most pious among you." (Quran 49:13) The wise, the pious, those knowledgeable in Islam and its true in practice are Islam's natural leaders.

To this end, within the structure of the Muslim faith, one finds the simple title of Scholar. The Scholar devotes many years of study of Islam. They cannot forgive sin, bless people or change the law of God. They are tasked with the job of passing on their knowledge by reference to the Quran and Sunnah, it is through their character that they inspire others.

There is no formal Clergy, no ordaining body, and no hierarchy. The relationship between the individual and God is a direct one. No one besides God can declare what is lawful and what is sinful. No created being can bless another. Each individual is directly accountable to his or her Lord and Creator. (**www.almasjid.com**)

Non-Abrahamic Faiths

Buddhism

The Buddhist faith, like most belief systems, has within it a number of variations. Many of these are based on cultural and/or geographical differences.

Buddhism was started in about the sixth century BCE by Siddhartha Gautama (Buddha Shakyamuni). He was born into the Royal Family Shakya (muni means "able one"). There were many predictions about his future in this world. At age twenty-nine, he retired to a forest in Bodh Gaya, India, to follow a spiritual life of meditation. After about six years, he attained enlightenment while seated under a Bodhi Tree (the symbol of this tree is still used in Buddhism).

His teachings included the "Four Noble (*Ârya*) Truths":

1) The truth of suffering, misery (*Duhkhasatya*). That life is suffering, including birth, disease, old age and death.

2 The truth of the cause (*Samudayasatya*). Suffering is caused by desire and ignorance (*avidyâ*) which ultimately depend on each other.

3) The truth of cessation (*Nirodhasatya*). That suffering can be ended if its causes, desires and ignorance are removed.

4) The truth of the way (*Mârgasatya*), which is the middle way between the extremes of asceticism and indulgence.

The "Eight Fold Way":

1) Right Knowledge (or Views), *samyagdr*
2) Right Resolve, *samyaksan.kalpa*
3) Right Speech, *samyagvâk*
4) Right Conduct (or Action), *samyakarma*
5) Right Livelihood, *samyagjîva*
6) Right Effort, *samyagvyâyâma*
7) Right Mindfulness, *samyaksmr*
8) Right Meditation (or Concentration), *samyaksamâdhi*

The Buddha created a monastic order (*the Sangha*) which had five precepts. These are not to kill, not to steal, not to be unchaste, not to drink intoxicants and not to lie. These precepts were to be followed by all Priests, Nuns and Lay People.

That the Buddha may originally have been just a person is not something extraordinary in Indian religion, where in Buddhism, Jainism, and Hinduism it is possible for *ordinary human beings* to become morally and spiritually superior to the Gods. Especially noteworthy is the belief that in achieving Enlightenment, the Buddha acquired supernatural powers.

Within the hierarchy of the Buddhist faith, you will find a bit of dissention as to position based on the sect you speak with. However, in Tibetan Buddhism it is essentially as follows:

At the pinnacle of religious and political power is the current incarnation of the Dalai Lama, directly following in status is the Panchen Lamas. Bodhisattvas denote the highest level of awareness (enlightenment) prior to full enlightenment, and exist with the vow that they will not enter the final stage of enlightenment until all living beings have entered it before them. In the monastic area are what can be referred to as meditators, these are the Monks and Nuns working to attain enlightenment, and serve the Temple in their daily lives.

Many wonder how the Dalai Lama is chosen, to put it quite

simply; he is not. The current Dalai Lama is considered the reincarnation of the previous Dalai Lama and ultimately the reincarnation or a manifestation of the Bodhisattva of Compassion, Avalokiteśvara. When the current Dalai Lama passes, the task of finding the location of reincarnation is begun. The search is the responsibility of the High Lamas of the Gelugpa tradition and the government of Tibet. It can take around two to three years (or more) to identify the new incarnation of the Dalai Lama.

The High Lamas conduct several rituals to increase the odds of finding the reincarnation quickly. They look for omens and seek hints in their dreams. They also devise tests for candidates they feel may be the reincarnation. Familiarity with the possessions of the previous Dalai Lama is considered the main sign of the reincarnation.

Having been found, the child is brought to Lhasa (or a similar location) for training in Buddhist thought and knowledge.

Hinduism

This term, used by so many, is not a singular religion. It is actually a term that has been used for a very long time to describe the various religious beliefs originating in the area of India (much like the words Paganism and Christianity are descriptors of the many paths in those beliefs). We will occasionally use this term as a base for the text on these religions to help with understanding.

While there is no evidence as to an individual who started the belief systems, all followers use the written *Sanatana Dharma (Eternal Text)*, this demonstrates that while there is no unified belief system or practices, their doctrine and practices are similar. Also found within the culture is the *Bhagavad Gita,* which is a spiritual text that encompasses all things that are related to human life on this plane of existence and is more of an epic story than a religious text. It does however; cover all of the requirements for right living within that belief system. Gandhi referred to this document as his spiritual dictionary.

The belief systems stemming from this religion have been considered among the oldest of all surviving beliefs. The followers of these paths consider it to be eternal, having no beginning. Each has remained essentially unchanged from its beginning. What is unique to the beliefs is there is no documentation that allows for the determination of who created each sect of these beliefs. What is known is they all seem to stem from the Vedic religion dating back to roughly 5500 BCE.

Vedic (Hindu)

The Vedic form developed the *Vedic Samhitas*: the *Rig-Veda, Sama-Veda* and the *Yajur-Veda*. The *Rig-Veda* is a collection of hymns dating to about 1500 BCE, while the other two comprise ceremonial details relating to sacrifice as they practiced it. The Gods of the *Rig-Veda* fall into two primary categories; the *Deva* were the Gods of nature and the *Asuras* who were the Gods of moral concepts. The *Deva* are usually considered younger than the *Asuras* (*Pūrve Devāh*). In later texts, the *Asuras* become demons. Keep in mind that this belief system views demons very differently than they are viewed by those outside of this particular culture.

The last surviving element of Vedism Is the *Srauta* tradition, which still follows many of the original principles of the Vedic religion and is prominent in Southern India.

Brahmanism (Hindu)

During the time period between the 10th and 6th centuries BCE, the *Mahajanapadas* developed from the *Rig-Vedic* tribes. It was during this time that the majority of the mantra portions of the Vedas were completed. It was also the time period that the Vedic Priesthood were organized into a number of schools (*Shakha*) and explanatory literature was created (thus the birth of the

Brahmanna). They edited the mantras and these mantras were preserved in purely oral format for about two thousand years.

There are a number of these beliefs, which we have not touched upon. It would be very difficult to cover each with the amount of information needed to give complete and accurate information. This would easily require a book unto itself. What I am providing here will give you a general concept of some of the various Hindu faiths and will help you to better understand the system as a whole.

Paganism

Paganism is another "umbrella" term for a very diverse group of beliefs. Each belief is unique unto itself, yet they are all quite similar in nature. In this section, we will briefly cover some of the history and touch on a few of the beliefs found within Paganism.

The word "Pagan" is derived from the Latin word *Pagus*, which essentially means "country dweller". This was originally used to describe people who lived outside the available reach of the main religion of the time and area. The interpretation of the word has change a great deal over time. It has become a word to describe just about anyone who does not follow one of the so-called "mainstream" religions.

It is believed that Pagan practice is among the oldest of all beliefs (in line with the Hindu faiths), but it is difficult to place an exact age because it has been handed down verbally through the centuries.

Found under this umbrella are a variety of beliefs, among them are Native American and Meso-American religions, Asatru and Odinism (Heathen beliefs), Druids and Wiccans, to name but a small few. While each of these beliefs has a strong individual foundation, there are a great many similarities to be found among most of the Pagan belief systems.

By and large, most of these beliefs place a strong emphasis on nature and the Earth, believing that it is our responsibility to sustain and maintain our surroundings in a way that will be both pleasing to the Divine, and allow for those things that have been provided to continue to flourish.

Paganism has been broken down even further into a sub-group that has been classified as "Neo-Pagan". This term was adopted with the resurgence of various ancient beliefs between 1950 and the mid 1970s. The term is used due to the lack of written history regarding the belief systems that fall within the category as well as the fact that there has been a merging of various aesthetics in the growth of some. Wiccans, Heathens and Druids have been placed in this category. This seems a bit unfair because they stem from some of the oldest beliefs known, but in all honesty, some have added more modern esoteric thought and/or removed certain aspects from the parent belief. This occurs throughout the religious world. Interpretation has great bearing on a religious philosophy (an example would be the 1,500 or so denominations found within Christianity or the various sects found in the Hindu faiths and within Buddhism).

Wicca

Most of the credit for the creation of Wicca is usually given to Gerald Gardner. While, historically, he did bring the Craft into the public eye shortly after the repeal of the Witch Laws of England in about 1949-50, it should be noted that his tradition was actually an extension of far older beliefs. Out of respect for his actions, he was brave enough to place the ancient practice of witchcraft in the light of mainstream society and, because of his work, many other practicing covens and traditions shortly followed suit. The term Wicca was not used to describe this practice until about 1951.

This is considered an Earth-Based belief system with heavy emphasis placed on the sanctity of all things sharing the planet. Over the course of years many aspects of other esoteric beliefs were added. This was primarily due to the similarities found between them and the practice of Wicca. As with all belief systems, Wicca is in a constant state of growth and flux.

Wicca has, over the years, encountered hardships; mostly due to myth and misconceptions about the past (almost all of which actually pre-date this practice). Many have worked hard at dispelling these myths and the belief has been recognized as a legitimate religion by the United States.

Found within Wicca are a number of traditions. These are larger groups, founded around a central practice as interpreted by its creator. Gardnerian, Alexandrian and Dianic Wicca are some examples. Traditions usually comprise of a group of Covens, Groves or Tribes who subscribe to specific denominational (for lack of a better word) belief.

These larger groups will often have common rituals, which are used by the various groups in membership. Many will hold annual festivals where all of the groups join together for a specific purpose.

A large percentage of the Wiccan community exists as solitary practitioners. These individuals prefer to raise their spiritual development in a more personal manner. Since the belief system has but one all-encompassing rule (Harm None), this allows for a broader view of Divinity and methods of practice. It is often said that one may share their path with others, but each must walk his or her own journey.

Druids

Often considered the oldest existing belief system, those on this path will often tell others that it is less a religion than a life journey. Although examples of Druidic existence dating back thousands of years can be found in virtually every corner of the globe, this path has only resurfaced in a prominent public aspect again since the early 1970s. The Druidic path has always been something of mystery simply because Druids do not seek the spotlight. In ages past, they have always been looked upon as the bards and educators.

Little is truly known of the history of this group, since it was carefully handed down verbally only to those who were accepted into the fold, or what has been translated from the many Ogham Standing Stones found mainly in Ireland. There is virtually no written documentation, save the "Standing Ogham Stones" and that which has been written since the 19th century. What we do know is that there are specific degrees of training and acknowledgement within this path and one is not truly considered a Druid until they have developed a degree of understanding by proceeding through all of those degrees.

In modern practice each practitioner begins his or her journey through Bardic training. This has its beginnings in ancient times when history was handed down in a verbal, storytelling or musical manner. This helps the beginner to develop their artistic and creative self. An individual can spend many years or an entire lifetime at this stage, perfecting their abilities and building a foundation for growth.

The second "degree" one will find is that of the Ovate. This, too, is a very lengthy journey which focuses on the natural path. Trees, herbalism and healing are the areas of intense training. Within Druidic culture, they are also the ones associated with the "other world" and are often found officiating during Samhain Rituals.

The final step is to become a Druid. This individual has devoted many years training in the first disciplines and has developed into a philosopher and teacher. Those outside the Druidic path often look at them as Priests and while they do preside over most Rituals, they are more directors of Ritual and see to it that those Rituals are maintained as they should be. They are looked upon for their wisdom and ability to teach those along the path.

Heathens

It is thought that this belief system originated in the Norse countries, but there is evidence that Heathens, like the Druids, had a heavy influence in most of the European Continent. They too, created Standing Stones, which use the Elder Futhark (a Germanic Rune, used for communication and divination).

Those who follow this belief are very firm in placing Family (both blood and extended) in the highest importance. They are also somewhat unique in the Pagan world due to the fact they do not look at the Gods and Goddesses as being facets of a singular Deity, but view each as a concrete being. In many of the historical tales surrounding this belief, it becomes apparent that these Gods and Goddesses possibly lived upon this Earth as humans and great heroes. Because of this status they rose to their present positions within the belief system.

Much of the belief has been garnered from epic tales found within its cultural roots; these stories were tales originally handed down verbally but were eventually put into writing.

In many circles, the title "Heathen" often brings up negative images due to its apparent influence within the Aryan Nation Organization and the early Nazi Party. Sadly, as with a number of beliefs, these thoughts get blown out of proportion and affect the belief badly. While these two groups have and do utilize some of the historical aspects of the Heathen culture, it is not a prevailing attitude and most who follow the Heathen path are found to be extremely honorable and strive to hold high the tenets of their belief.

Common Misconceptions Surrounding Religion

There are many myths and misconceptions associated with belief systems considered to be outside the mainstream. These myths were created in a time when, in an effort to convert others, the so-called "reigning" Church of the time used a great deal of propaganda as a tool to create distrust. This tool was used to attempt to force others to disavow their traditional beliefs and follow theirs. Many of these myths began in the early 1200s at the beginning of the infamous Inquisition; others have developed in our more modern era. It is not the design of this section to create animosity, but rather point out how a number of things have turned the truth into something less. These myths and misconceptions are not just directed at those following a Pagan path, but some have been created or grown through misinterpretation or misinformation about various belief systems.

First, we will look at a term from outside the Pagan culture in an effort to demonstrate how a simple word can be used as a trigger for misunderstanding and hatred. The word is "Jihad". Most people hear this word and immediately envision Muslim terrorists; and sadly it has become accepted to mean that. However, if you were to read the Quran, you would see this word used a number of times throughout the text and not once is it used to demonstrate any acts of violence. It is used to demonstrate the non-violent inner struggle toward duty to God or worship of God and carries no violent connotations. The word used to demonstrate violent acts is "Qital". The violent aspect given to the term Jihad came from an interpretive definition developed by the US Department of Justice during the indictments of a number of active terrorists.

For a very long time, a five-pointed star was (and in some cases, still is) used in many faiths as a symbol. This star or Pentagram has been used and is still in use by many belief systems as well as being a symbol on many national flags (about 25% of the world's flags) and is often used this way as a connection to God. Very early in Christianity, this icon was used to demonstrate the five stripes suffered by Christ on the cross. In the Pagan culture it is often referred to as the Star of Venus and is almost always displayed pointing upward. It also has been used as a representation of the five primary elements in Earth-Based belief; Earth, Air, Fire, Water and Spirit. The symbol is still used by the Freemasons Order of the Eastern Star and is found as a religious icon within the Mormon Church. It is also used as the military Medal of Honor. These last three display it point down. The acceptance of a negative value only became prevalent with the advent of modern Satanism (the church of Satan was announced in 1966).

The thought that Pagans or witches worship Satan actually started in the middle ages as a method of dehumanizing them in the eyes of the general population, thereby allowing for the many acts of violence perpetrated on those who were originally thought of as healers. Pagans (as well as a majority of the world's belief systems) do not acknowledge the idea or existence of Satan or Hell as they are defined by Christian beliefs. The Pagan culture believes that both light and dark exist in all things and this is needed to create both balance and free will.

There are far more myths and misconceptions than are listed here and if you research the subject, you will find that these myths exist in and about virtually all beliefs. Most stem from the fact that these beliefs are misunderstood in one way or another and a stigma has been applied to them through ignorance and lack of research. It was once said that what man does not understand, he attempts to destroy; these words have great value. As practitioners of our path, we should always strive to understand, not condemn, and as such, should take the time to learn and grow.

Interfaith Bridging

In order to carry a positive action we must develop here a positive vision.
Dalai Lama

The need for understanding and cooperation
In our modern society, the need for understanding and

co-operation has become paramount. There was a time, not so long ago, when our world seemed very large. With the rising population, advent of social networks via the internet and the ease of interconnectivity this creates, our world has become quite small.

We went through a short period of religious tolerance, but once again, religious and social bigotry has started to raise its head. There are many who have found that the ability to reach a larger audience is a means to teach intolerance and hate, which violates the concepts of virtually every belief system on earth. In many cases the media has used this as a springboard to twist the views of people. Tactics very similar to the misinformation spread centuries ago by religious zealots now have the power to reach multitudes. It is the duty of Clergy to represent their belief in the manner taught at the beginning, but this is not always the case.

It is our job to promote the positive, not spread rumor. We need to learn about the teachings of other faiths. By doing this, we will begin to have a greater understanding, which will aid us in creating a positive environment. It is not our job to try to change anyone's belief or religious view, but it is our job to live and act in a way that demonstrates we are firm in our devotion to the Divine.

It is important that we realize that there are those in the world who would use any means possible to create conformity to their belief. Historically, and sadly on the rise once again, this includes violence. But it is also important to know that there are just as many, if not more, who hold true to their faith and practice compassion and understanding. It is the more radical factions of religion who are the most vocal in their assault of other faiths (and this too is found in absolutely every belief). If one is comfortable with his/her faith, it is not necessary to expound the virtue of it, no need to try to assimilate others into their culture.

It is impossible to prove beyond any shadow of doubt that any single belief is the "one true way", we all act on faith. Most forget what the word faith means; it is defined as a *"firm belief in something for which there is no absolute proof: complete trust"*. Based on this definition, we must strive to understand as much as we can and use that knowledge as a platform for growth. It has been said that life is a journey and each must walk his own path, this is a very true statement and one, as members of the Clergy, we must remember and work to live by.

Interfaith Organizations

A word of warning when determining if you and your group want to be a part of an interfaith organization, combination titles should raise a yellow flag, terms such as Pagan interfaith or Christian interfaith may be perfectly innocent and truly devoted to developing open understanding and acceptance. However, in many cases they are working to bring groups and individuals on board in an attempt to "bring them around" to their way of thinking. Yes, I did mention Pagan interfaith; there are a few groups out there that I have watched claim to be "interfaith", yet have seen them make many disparaging statements about belief systems not their own. This action is definitely not an interfaith value.

The majority of these organizations are truly working on positive interfaith practices, but it is always wise to research a group's ideals and policies before committing to work with them. If this seems a bit distrustful, it is to a degree. In this modern age, it is easy to find those who will use facades to achieve a goal. By knowing what a particular group stands for, you become far less likely to be taken in.

A few things to look for:

- Single minded or strictly linear thinking ("this is the only way to believe").
- Leadership that points the way, disallowing any input

outside of their own thoughts.
- Use of stigmas to define other beliefs.

If you encounter any of these or similar ideals, it is probably a good idea to stay away from them.

Phase 6: Applied Ritual Practice

Sacred spaces can be created in any environment.
Christy Turlington

Over the centuries, Ritual practices have changed significantly. Some would actually say that modern Ritual practice has become a somewhat lazy and lackadaisical venture, falling short of the respect levels needed for successful Ritual.

There are a number of misconceptions about what Ritual really is. The term is often used for the opening of an event or something similar. *This is not a Ritual!* It is for all intents and purposes simply an invocation. Ritual has a much more profound meaning and value. Ritual is a depiction of a relevant event surrounding the mythos (theology) of a given belief system which is used to raise needed energy for other practical applications (i.e.; Magickal practice) prior to the releasing of the Circle.

The preparations used today include a number of shortcuts, which could be viewed as irresponsible or possibly dangerous when compared to the older ways.

In this section, we will compare a complete and thorough preparation style and modern practices. The goal is to teach you the differences and the values (or lack of) of each. The American Spiritual Alliance works to teach the need for proper preparation and the value of showing proper respect in order to create a significantly more effective Sacred Space and therefore a more successful Ritual.

Choosing and Preparing the Sacred Space

The first, and most important aspect of your preparation, is choosing the location of your Sacred Space. You should be sure that the location is large enough to both sustain the space and contain the attendees (be that number small or large). It was once considered vital that the space be such that those in attendance have enough room to move about but not inadvertently leave the space, breaking the Circle and rendering the space unusable. This is not always an easy task to accomplish. In many cases today, our Rituals are performed indoors and adequate space is at a premium. Most groups will need to rent a location and this is not inexpensive. The larger the space, the more it will cost. This has caused many groups to sacrifice the thought of not breaking the Circle and employing the idea that the Circle would be completely protected by the Guardians. As we progress, hopefully, you will come to see that it is the practitioner's responsibility to maintain the Sacred Space and not the responsibility of any elemental or divine entity.

In times past, most Rituals were held outside, which made it much easier to find an appropriately sized location. Modern practitioners are often somewhat leery of public Ritual due to the influence of social pressures. In other cases, the potential for inclement weather presents an issue. On this subject, let us remember, ours is a path based on nature and the elements. It is sad to think that we would require an element-free environment for the practice of our belief. In all but the worst environmental conditions, our predecessors would gather for Ritual in full contact with all of the elements. It is this contact that helps to vitalize our Ritual and enhances the participation of Deity.

OK, you have found a location that will adequately meet your needs. Now the real work begins. It is time to prepare the Sacred Space for use.

Today it is quite common to set up our Altar, mark the four quarters and proceed to casting the Circle. This could be due to our rushed lifestyle. We are essentially slaves to time. We tend to wait until the last minute to be ready for most things. This is not limited to our path, but also is a basic part of our daily lives. Modern society tends to try to time things to such a point that we will arrive at work with mere seconds to spare; leaving no time for issues that may arise. When we arrive late to an event or our event starts late because something did not go as planned, we fall back on something that has become far too common in our world. Sorry to say it, but "fashionably late" and "Pagan Central Time" are insulting, even though it is rare that anything is ever said to prevent them. We have allowed ourselves to accept these so-called time issues as normal and acceptable and, because of this, we have allowed many shortcuts to become commonplace. Taking these shortcuts sets our Sacred Space up for some very serious issues.

The preparation of your space should be completed prior to any attendees arriving and the space should be declared off limits to anyone until it is time to begin your Ritual. This is very important because anyone entering the space prior to the Ritual leader inviting attendees into the Circle will destroy all of the preparatory work you have done.

Proper preparation of the space includes a great deal more than simply placing items and casting a Circle. The very first step in preparing your space is preparing yourself. If you even begin to prepare your Sacred Space without first cleansing your spiritual energies, any negative energy surrounding you will affect your space. This will negate your Circle and make it quite useless. There are steps you should take to avoid this happening, but you must first realize that these steps take time and trying to shorten them will affect the overall outcome. Do not rush, follow the steps and you will create something both valuable and powerful.

It is vital to Ground and Center. In doing this, you will be releasing negative energy from within yourself and clearing your mind so that you can be more focused on the remaining tasks. Depending on the situation or mood, this process can be either simple or lengthy. Regardless of which type you employ, it is vital that at the completion of your Grounding and Centering you should feel the positive energies within yourself. Once you have done this, it is suggested that you purify and cleanse your Aura; this can be done with a simple smudging. Most who use this technique will use sage as the appropriate cleanser. Smudging does not limit you to a smoke smudging; it can be done with a spray made of essential oils (*this is brought up because there are many people who can have a severe reaction to the smoke emanating from a smudge stick*).

In an effort to allow Deity to act more effectively through you, take the time to enter your Higher Self. This entails the elevation of the energy frequency of your body to more readily align with the Divine. Entering your Higher Self is a time-consuming task, but is very important to enhancing your Ritual's effectiveness as well as ensuring the effective preparation of your space.

This process is necessary to allow for the cleansing of your space. If you are allowing others to assist in the preparation, they too should follow the same process. It is also suggested that, whenever possible, those who are chosen to assist be on the path to obtaining Clergy status or are currently members of the Clergy. The training that they have received will help them to better understand the need to be thorough in the process. If this is not possible, it is the duty of the Ritual leader to train, advise and oversee those who will participate. This should be done well in advance of the Ritual.

The time has come to actually begin the process of readying the Sacred Space for use. As was said earlier, many will simply place items to be used within the space and cast the Circle. Doing this will not allow the space to be placed between the worlds and this will, again, render the Circle useless. It will also leave any and all types of energy within the space and this could be a recipe for disaster. Take care and follow the cleansing process completely and you will likely have a very positive Ritual.

Cleansing the Sacred Space

First, you must completely clear the space of all negative energy.

This may be accomplished in a number of ways. For the purposes of this class, we will cover but a few of the more effective methods.

Clearing by Besom

Using this process is quite effective, but is also quite time consuming, depending on the size of your Sacred Space.

First of all, the Besom must be blessed and Charged for this duty. Failing to do this, the Besom will have no effect on the space at all. A cinnamon Besom is an excellent choice because cinnamon is a naturally protective substance.

Now, working from the center of your space, sweep the area completely working continually outward in a circular manner (sort of in a spiral pattern, more or less). The bristles of the Besom should never make contact with the ground or floor (the energies are drawn to the Besom like a magnet). Make sure that you cover every part of the space completely; all negative energy must be expelled from within. During this process, you might use a chant to aid in expelling negativity and securing positive energy. Chanting has been common in Ritual for many centuries and is a most effective tool.

Once you have completed sweeping the area, place the Besom outside of the space so that it may be recharged at a later time. Under no circumstances should the Besom re-enter the space until it has been recharged; nor should it be used to clear any other area until it has been recharged. This is because this tool is designed to absorb and cast out negative energy and as such, bringing it back into the space could release those negative energies back into the space. You might also consider using salt to reground and clear yourself prior to re-entering the space. A simple bowl containing salt placed just outside the space will work just fine. Simply take a small handful of the salt and simulate washing your hands with it and allowing the salt to fall back into the bowl. Care should be taken to not spill any of the salt inside the space because it now contains any negative energy that you may have picked up from the Besom.

Clearing by Smudging

The use of smudging is a cleansing technique that has been used around the world for many centuries and by a great many cultures. It is a simple process, but care must be taken when choosing exactly what herb to use for the task. Each herb has specific properties and can initiate a cause and effect situation. With this in mind, if your Ritual has definite intent, you might research what smudging herb would be most conducive to achieving it. As a general cleansing herb, white sage is often considered universal in use. The primary properties of white sage are cleansing and protection, which makes it well suited for use in preparing your Sacred Space.

A simple method of clearing a space by smudging uses two objects to complete the task, a feather that has been charged to the purpose and the smudge stick (these are commercially available or can be easily made by the practitioner).

You will begin by lighting the smudge stick while standing in the center of your chosen space. You begin moving around the Circle creating a spiral outward to the outer edge of the space. While you work your way around the Circle, use the feather to spread the smoke outward, filling the area with the purifying powers of the smudge stick. As in the Besom process, a chant may be used to banish negativity from your space. Once you have completed this process, douse the smudge stick and place it somewhere outside the Circle. Unlike the Besom technique, it is not necessary to recharge or bless either of these items as they do not absorb any negative energy. They actually drive the negative energy out of your space while filling it with a protective energy that is coupled with the remaining positive energy.

Clearing by Water

This method requires advance preparation because you will need to create Holy Water and this is something that can require a number of days to make and is a very involved process. The most important part of this process is the making of the Holy Water, the remainder of the cleansing is virtually identical to the smudging process. It is recommended that this technique be used by an advanced practitioner, one who has training in the area of making potions.

Following is a method I use for the creation of Holy Water.

Formula for Holy Water

1 tsp. of rose water (optional)

3 tbs. sea salt

1 small bowl of spring water

1 clean glass container

1 small mirror

1 storage bottle (large enough to contain the liquid after preparation)

Time: Midnight during a full moon phase.

Place: Out of doors under the moon, or near a window that will reflect the light of the moon.

Cleanse and sterilize the bowl and glass container with boiling water. Ensure that you have total privacy during preparation. Set out your Altar cloth and place all of the ingredients upon it. You should have already entered your Higher Self by this point.

Cast your Sacred Space, if you do not have a permanent space for these purposes. Hold your arms outstretched in the Goddess position (arms out at the sides like you are cradling the Universe, palms up). Say:

In the cloak of the midnight hour
I call upon the Ancient Power

I seek the presence of the Lady and Lord
To bless this water that I will pour.

At this point, you should feel the energy of the Lord and Lady move about your feet and head. Feel your own energy expand around your navel and then unite with Divinity. Take your time; no need to rush. Add the rose water to the spring water. Pick up the bowl of water, hold it toward the light of the moon. Say:

In my hands I hold the essence of the Gods. I hereby cleanse and consecrate this water to Divinity that it may be used for positive acts only and may aid me in my Magickal work.

Feel the energy of the Moon Goddess pulsate down into the water. Imagine her silver light descending from the heavens and entering both the water and yourself. You will feel a somewhat electrical vibration in your body. Set the water down and pick up the salt. Feel the power moving in your arms as you raise the salt to the moon. Say:

In my hands I hold the essence of Earth Mother, She whose bounty sustains all living creatures.

I hereby consecrate this salt to Divinity that it may be used for positive acts only and may aid me in my Magickal work.

As with the water, imagine the energy of the Moon Goddess empowering the salt. Set the salt down and pour a little into the bowl of water, and stir clockwise three times.

With the bowl in your left hand (receiving) and the mirror in your right (sending), reflect the light of the moon off the mirror and into the bowl. Allow the moon's energy a little time before proceeding. Say:

This liquid is now pure and dedicated to the Lord and Lady.

It is free from all negativity in any time and any space.

Set the bowl and mirror down and hold both of your hands, palms down, over (not touching) the bowl, about one inch above the water. Let the vibrations of your body come alive. Imagine a glowing purple light emanating from you. Form an open triangle with your hands over the water and project the light into it. In your mind, see the water change color and glow. Feel the power and energy flow from your head down through your arms and up from your feet and out from your arms simultaneously. When you feel the energy begin to dissipate, slowly lower your hands.
Say:

As I will
So mote it be
With the free will of all
And harm to none
This formula is done!

You should release the built up energy. Place your hands physically upon the ground and feel the energy drain into Earth Mother, this will allow those energies to be available to you again at a later time. Transfer the water to your storage container and store it away until you are ready to cleanse and consecrate your Sacred Space.

Placing the Altar and Tools

With our space clear, we can now advance to the placement of any of the items we will be using during the Ritual. These items will include our Altar, Altar tools, Guardian symbols, etc. As with all things, it is very important to the success of your Ritual that every object be blessed and charged for the purpose of Ritual. Your Ritual items should never be used for any other purpose or they will require a complete recleansing to make them Ritual ready. One vital note, your Athame must never have been used to cut anything or have drawn blood of any kind. It is symbolic of the God, not a cutting knife and should never be used for that purpose. If an item needs to be cut, it should be done with your Boline (a separate knife kept for preparing ingredients used for Magickal purposes).

Placing the Altar sounds like a very simple task, doesn't it? In most cases it is. The Altar is often placed on the North end of your Sacred Space. But this is not always the case. In some Rituals, your intent is specific to a certain elemental power and it may be prudent to place the Altar so that it is in proximity to that element. Doing this will enhance the energy and power of your Ritual and in all likelihood improve the outcome of the Ritual. If you choose to use this method for placing your Altar (and even if you just decide to place it to the North), a compass might be a good addition to your non-Magickal Altar supplies.

We are all aware of what Altar tools should attend a Ritual. However, after many years of attending Rituals around the country, it has become painfully obvious that many just arrange their tools on the Altar table so that they are visible or look aesthetically pleasing and ignore the fact that there is a great deal of symbolic value to the Altar table. While most traditions do in fact teach about Altar symbolism, it seems that many let the importance of this fall by the wayside. Even this can have a great effect on the outcome of your Ritual.

The Altar table is historically divided into two sides; the left side is symbolic of the feminine aspect of Deity, while the right side is the masculine aspect. Altars tools should be placed in a location on the table that corresponds with the nature of the tool. By doing this, your tools will be further empowered and this in turn enhances the effectiveness of your Ritual.

In today's world, many do not mark the quarters of their Circle or Sacred Space. This may be done because of space constraints, lack of time or lack of thought. Regardless of the reason, not marking the quarters can have adverse consequences on your Ritual. Marking the quarters serves a couple of purposes. First, it makes it much easier for the Ritual leader to properly call the quarters. The most important reason is it is a demonstration of respect and allows for the placement of an appropriate offering for the individual elementals. Failing to provide for this (especially if you consistently fail to provide this), can lead to the elemental guardians choosing not to attend and provide the requested protection during the event. Once again, this can have disastrous effects on your Ritual.

After all of this work, you now have a properly protected and energized Sacred Space. While the process is very time consuming, you will find your Rituals will be greatly improved through the use of these methods. Now and only now is your space ready for you to call the Circle.

Calling the Circle

When Calling the Circle, it can be quite simple to very elaborate; this is entirely up to the host. There are, however, a number of aspects to this task that are of great importance. In this section we will be using a technique for the Calling as an example. Many people will create their own method of Calling the Circle and this is fine, as a matter of fact. If properly done this can add a great deal of impact to your Ritual. Do not discount the value of taking the time to create your own Calling.

Prior to Calling the Circle, the Ritual leader needs to properly Ground and Center as well as take time to invoke their Higher Self. Yes, you did do this prior to the preparation of your space, however; you have spent time outside the space and time has allowed the potential of gathering negative energy which must be dissipated to allow for successful Ritual.

Your first decision when Calling the Circle is, will your Calling be performed prior to the admission of the attendees or will you allow those in attendance entrance so that they may witness the process? This is entirely up to the host, but each carries with it certain facets which must be maintained.

If your Circle is to be called prior to the admission of your guests, you will need adequate assistance for the Circle to remain intact. Anyone coming into the Circle will need to be cleansed of negative energy and this will require having Acolytes just outside the space to either smudge or water cleanse those preparing to enter the space (this means each and every individual). Failure to do this will allow any negativity carried by your guests to enter the Sacred Space and essentially disassemble the Circle from the inside out. Keep in mind, this does not just affect the Material Plane, but can also have impact on the Astral Plane (your Circle, once created, rests between these two Planes). Think about the potential consequences of this occurring. Using this method also requires you to cut an entrance into the space for your guests to pass through. It additionally encumbers the Ritual leader because he/she must be present at the entrance of the space so that they can feel any negative emanations of the people entering (remember that the Ritual leader is currently in his/her Higher Self and is much more in tune with negative vibrations). This creates a possibly challenging situation that may not be received very well.

There are many risks involved in Calling the Circle before admitting anyone and generally it is not an advisable practice. This also includes beginning the process prior to and during admittance of the guests as is found among some traditions. Laying the foundation for a strong Sacred Space is vital to the success of the Ritual.

Should you choose to allow guests to witness the Calling, the entrance process is just slightly less demanding, but not much.

A few minutes prior to allowing your guests to enter the space, you should instruct them to Ground and Center so that any negative vibrations may be cast off. If you have attendees who are not familiar with the process, you should be prepared to assist them in this aspect of the Ritual. Always keep in mind that not everyone has attended Ritual before and because of this, you should have people who are trained to assist them. It is also a good idea to advise them, at this point, that they should enter the space quietly and to remain quiet during the Ritual unless there is a responsive aspect included in the Ritual. If there is, your assistants should know when this is and start the response.

When the time has come, your Acolytes should lead the guests into the space. Guests should never be allowed to just walk all over the place. They should be guided around the perimeter until the space is occupied by all those attending. Should anyone need reasonable accommodation because of a disability, those needs should be handled at this time. Once again, you should anticipate the possibility of these needs and be prepared for them. Prior to Calling the Circle, the Acolytes should walk the Circle and either smudge or water cleanse the attendees. In this method, you can easily cleanse all in attendance quickly and easily. Using this technique allows for guests to enter in a much more organized and expedient manner and also allows the Ritual leader the opportunity to further align their Higher Self to Deity.

Having all this done, it is now time to actually Call the Circle. There are as many ways to Call the Circle as there are followers of the path. Because ours is a path that allows for individuality, many practitioners have developed their own methods. The primary concerns when Calling the Circle are demonstrating respect for Deity and the elemental guardians, respect for the space and those in attendance and recognition that this process is a very spiritual act.

When Calling the Quarters, you should always request respectfully that the elemental guardians join your Circle and place an offering that symbolizes each of them. Possible offerings would include incense for Air, a candle for Fire, etc. These offerings are not only symbolic, but important in demonstration of spiritual respect.

Deity should also be asked to empower your Altar. This is quite important, since all Ritual is a demonstration of the respect of the Divine. Never shortcut any act that is directed to the Divine, to do so is an affront to Deity and will not be well received.

The Circle is now created and sits safely between two worlds. You may proceed to the main Ritual. This can be centered on any number of intents, but should always be of a positive nature, focused on doing no harm. As a final note, no one should ever be allowed to just walk out of the Sacred Space, it is wise to station an Acolyte at the exit point and have them open a doorway for exit and close it immediately upon an individual's departure. Constant exiting and returning is a disruption and once a person steps out of the space, they should not be allowed re-entry because the cleansing process must be redone in an effort to retain the integrity of the Circle (you may want to advise those in attendance of this prior to their initial entrance into the space). Some groups go as far as to station Acolytes outside the Circle to bar entry after Ritual has began in an effort to keep any negative energy outside the space. This is not necessarily a bad idea.

Releasing the Circle

At the end of your Ritual, your tasks are not quite complete. Before any of your guests are allowed to leave the Sacred Space, the Circle must be closed. Failing to do this can, as stated before, affect both the Material Plane and the Astral Plane, bringing potentially disastrous results. It is your duty to complete the Ritual by closing the Circle in both a respectful and proper manner. This is often the most neglected aspect of Ritual and is sometimes considered a simple afterthought; but this is definitely not the case. It is singularly as important as any other step in the Ritual process.

The Ritual leader should approach each quarter and take the

time to thank each elemental Deity and release them from their post. It is also vital that he/she thank the Divine for their attendance and their blessing of the Ritual. They graced you with both their presence and their blessing so it is most appropriate that you thank them both honestly and accordingly. Releasing the Guardians begins the process of moving the Circle from between two worlds back onto the Material Plane. As with the Calling the Circle, the wording can be prepared by the host, but as with everything found in this process, certain aspects must never be left out. To shortcut anything is to ask for failure.

If you have any candles lit, do not blow them out. Blowing out a candle can be considered a demonstration of lack of respect. Extinguish any candles using a snuffer; this is demonstrative of proper decorum and respect.

As most Circles are closed, a common incantation is: "*The Circle is closed but never broken*". The accompanying response would be: "*So mote it be*". The leader may then make a short statement and then allow the guests to leave the Circle, led out by the Acolytes that brought them into the Circle.

As you have probably learned at this point, each step leading to and ending the main Ritual are small Rituals themselves. Each step is important and no step should be bypassed. To achieve a truly positive outcome means following all the steps to ensure that all things are in place and Deity is in attendance.

It is incumbent on the host to see to it that nothing adversely affects your Ritual and by providing adequate personnel you can assure a positive and powerful outcome to your event. Whether the event is something positive or negative to talk about is purely up to the hosting group. It is your job to present your group and tradition in a positive manner and simply by following designs provided by centuries of practice and patience will help to ensure that it will be considered a positive event.

Creating a Ritual

The creation of a Ritual is something every member of the Clergy should learn. While it is not an easy project, it is both very satisfying and empowering to perform a Ritual which has been written by you.

As with most aspects of our path, you need to open yourself to the Divine. Doing this will allow Deity to guide you in this creation; it will also embody the Ritual with both your energy and the energy derived through Deity.

Ritual is a form of Magickal practice as well as Energy Raising and as such there must be intent. In the creative process, the first question you must ask yourself is, "What is my purpose? What is it I wish to achieve?" Whether it is a Ritual for a group or a personal Ritual prepared for no one else to see or use, there must be a goal. It does not have to be a lofty, involved goal; it could be as simple as calling upon Deity to make a Magickal herb garden flourish. This would constitute a minor Ritual, unlike a public one which will be covered next. The two are quite different in both design and use.

You have your intent, now comes the real work. We will focus on public/group Ritual for this section because these are a bit more "theatrical" and formal in nature. When a Ritual is performed in a public arena, it takes on a performance art aspect. It must be created in a way that projects energy into your attendees, this allows their energy to mingle with the intent and amplify it, promoting the potential of a much more positive outcome.

The information you learned in Ritual preparation applies to the creation of your Ritual. How will you prepare the Sacred Space? Will it be done in private, prior to the arrival of your attendees? Or will you choose to make this a part of the overall Ritual? If it is to be done as a unified part of your Ritual, this would need to be scripted into your project (this includes anyone you enlist to help you). Here, we might add the thought that in using a public area, clearing of the space comes with its own set of problems. Any negativity can not only slow, but also actually render the space unusable. It is usually preferable to arrive early and set yourself to clearing it in private and maintaining a perimeter so that people do not just walk into it prior to the completion of your Ritual. Clearing the Sacred Space takes time and is not necessarily the most entertaining part to watch, remember, the goal is to build positive energy within the Circle.

Err on the side of caution, always include *all* of the aspects you have learned for clearing the Circle, do not take shortcuts. Benjamin Franklin said, "He who fails to plan, plans for failure." Very wise words indeed, for if you do not prepare accordingly (this includes allowing time for the process to be done completely), your Ritual will be nothing more than words, having no impact on the intent whatsoever. If there are time constraints, you should act accordingly by arriving early to properly clear the space you will be using in private.

Regardless of the timing used to lead attendees into the Circle, as they enter they should be cleansed of negative energy. This can be done by some manner of asperging, be it with blessed water (making this was taught during your First Degree training) or smudging (remember what we learned about smudging techniques).

Calling the quarters is next. Is this aspect to be seen by your attendees, or will you choose to have them assembled in a location which will allow them to hear the Circle being called? Both of these are acceptable. If properly done, placing your attendees in a position to hear, but not see, the Circle being called tends to build energy. Taking this course, however, requires someone with a strong voice and great conviction. Keep in mind; this is not license to merely read from a script. To do so would be an affront to the Divine, the Guardians, you and the attendees. If it is lacking in any of these areas, it would be wise to choose having the attendees present at the Circle.

There are many ways to call the quarters, but remember, to not call the quarters leaves your Circle unprotected and lacking the energies provided by the Ancient Ones. Many, when calling the quarters, will call upon the Dragons of the Watch Towers. While this is an acceptable method; it is used so often, by so many, that it sometimes is perceived as a lack of conviction and intent. The method of calling the Dragons been adapted and adopted from an ancient practice called the Dragon Rituals. It is simply my opinion that this method should only be used when performing that type of Ritual and nowhere else. It is here that you need to be open to Deity to lend a guiding hand in the process of Ritual creation.

An Example of Calling the Circle

This method can be used in both of the styles we discussed earlier. While you are free to use this example, which was written by Rev. Rosenblad, it is put here simply to provide you with an idea of how to create this portion of your Ritual. As you will see, it is written in a very script-like fashion. This allows for any directions needed to be understood by all who play a part in your Ritual.

You, the High Priest (or designee), face the Altar at the center of the intended Circle, and say: *"I create this Circle that it may rest in the space between worlds and contain all the energies raised within."*

Begin to move in a clockwise direction around the Circle, with the Athame or other chosen tool directed toward the outer edge of the Circle boundary, and say: *"I consecrate this Circle to be a barrier of protection against all that is contrary to my will and intent."*

Return to the Altar and pause in reverent silence for a moment. Raise the Athame above your head and say, *"I call upon the Elemental Guardians to attend this Circle that we may share in their energy and power."*

Move to the Northern quarter of the space (holding the Athame in front of the body, point up); point the Athame toward the Northern quarter and create the shape of the pentagram in a clockwise manner with the Athame. Say, *"From the North, I call upon the Ancient one of the Earth. Join our Circle that we may feel your wisdom and knowledge kindle within."* Place the appropriate offering in the North quarter.

Move to the Eastern quarter as before, again creating the pentagram, and say, *"Ancient one of the East, Guardian of Air, the very breath of life, join our Circle. Grant us your power that we may grow and understand."* Again, place the appropriately chosen offering at the Eastern quarter.

Move to the Southern quarter, recreate the pentagram as before. Say, *"Ancient Guardian of the South, bearer of Fire, strength and energy we ask that you join our Circle and share your power that our intent be strengthened."* Place the appropriate offering at the Southern quarter.

Move to the Western quarter, creating the shape of the pentagram once more. Say, *"Guardian of the West, join our Circle and share with us the power of the element of Water that our Circle be made pure and clean."* Place the offering at the Western quarter.

Slowly move around the edge of the Circle, Athame directed to the outer edge. Say, *"The Guardians are present, the Circle is cast. May all done this day be in Perfect Love and Perfect Trust... So Mote It Be."*

Move once again to the Altar, place the Athame in its proper place and remain in a moment in silence. The Ritual may now begin.

Releasing the Circle bears the same importance as Calling the Circle and should never be disregarded. Failing to properly release the Circle can have serious repercussions, unless of course it is a permanent Ritual location and not available to general public access. Even if it is permanent, it must still be closed, but under these circumstances your closing will somewhat different. In closing a permanent space, the Circle is not dissipated (released) as it would be at a public venue because through repetitive use the space builds up and contains positive energies that will only add to the power of Ritual. You must in all cases release the Guardians to return to their realm; failure to do this demonstrates a lack of respect to the importance of the elemental balance.

Following is a sample of a simple (yet respectful) release for a Circle in a public location. The release of the Guardians is sufficient for the permanent Ritual space.

You, or the HP, moves to the West quarter of the Circle, directing the Athame at a slightly upward angle, and says, *"We thank you, ancient one of the West for your presence. We release you with admiration. Blessings and farewell."*

Move to the South quarter, Athame still in an upward position. Say, *"We thank you, ancient one of the South for your presence. We release you with admiration. Blessings and farewell."*

Move to the East quarter with the Athame positioned as before. Say, *"We thank you ancient one of the East for your presence. We release you with admiration. Blessings and farewell."*

Move to the North quarter. Say, *"We thank you ancient one of the North for your presence. We release you with admiration. Blessings and farewell."*

Walk slowly, counterclockwise, around the perimeter of the Circle, Athame directed to the outer edge of the Circle. Say, *"I release this Circle and return both halves to their own realm. May the energies created this day be carried within each of us."* Move to the center of the space. Say, *"The Circle has been closed but remains unbroken. Go now in peace and understanding. Blessed Be."*

While calling the quarters and releasing the Circle are vital to the overall success of your Ritual, they are by far the easiest parts to create. To create and place into use a Ritual of your own design is quite involved and very difficult for someone just beginning their journey. Most will opt for an accepted prepared Ritual because of this.

In the creation of an actual Ritual, there are a number of

factors involved that *cannot* be ignored.

Primary to all Ritual is the fact that each one contains a reflection of the theologies and ideologies of your tradition, in effect; Ritual is somewhat of a pageant relating the story of a specific theological event. For example, your Ritual might be focused on the Wheel of the Year, detailing the intertwining of the God and Goddess through the Sabbats and Esbats.

The first thing you must keep in mind is, you are essentially writing a script that, when performed, tells a specific story based on the belief system you follow. Some belief systems call them "Passion Plays", but in reality they are Ritual acts of respect for a given event through re-enactment.

With these things firmly in mind, you can now begin. What aspect of your belief system are you planning to show? Will it be one of the Quarter Days or Cross-Quarter Days, or perhaps the Wheel itself? Maybe the Descent of the Goddess. Whatever you decide on, make sure you have detailed knowledge of the event or events you are depicting. Now that you have your focus, you can move on to the creation of your Ritual.

Remember, you are relating a story pertinent to your belief. It must be empowered and engaging so that it is able to raise the energies of those attending the Circle. This will pave the way for any Magickal aspects to follow the primary Ritual. Prior to the actual Ritual, many use chanting or drums to build energy within the Circle. Raising energy in this way has a profound effect on the Ritual itself.

Do not simply choose a subject for your creation; you must have passion if it is to be successful. Open yourself to the Divine for guidance. Allow her hand to direct you to that which will have power.

In preparing the script for the Ritual, the timing must be smooth and flow like water. Do not bounce around; recreate the sequence of events so they blend seamlessly. Maintain a balanced storyline; do not create a trampoline that jumps from one subject to the next.

Writing a powerful Ritual requires imagery, this does not always mean visual, it should be written in a way that produces vivid mental images of the subject as well. This too will raise the level of energy and power within the Circle.

Once you feel your creation is complete, have a fellow member of the Clergy read it. Find out if it causes them to not only understand what you have put forth, but to feel and see in their mind what it is you are relating. If they cannot, your work is not done and you should try to find the source of the issue.

As was said earlier, many choose to use proven prepared Rituals. To write a Ritual for presentation is an arduous task and not something everyone can accomplish. It takes a great deal of time, experience and passion to create a successful Ritual.

Using a Prepared Ritual

I will caution you here before you begin searching for possible Rituals. When using a prepared Ritual that is not commonly used by a tradition (*found on the internet or some other questionable source*), be cautious. Read the Ritual with a critical eye and ask; does it address my intent? Does it pay proper respect to Deity? Does it meet the standards of Ritual practice for our tradition?

There are a great many prepared Rituals available that have been in use for a long time, our tradition also maintains a library of Rituals that are available to our Clergy members. It is vital that you remember that if you choose to use a prepared Ritual, particularly one commonly used by another tradition, it is either in Public Domain (not a currently copyrighted work), or you have express (preferably written) permission to use it. Sadly, even among those on our path, we live in a litigious society and all efforts must be taken to avoid legal issues.

The Priest's Role in Ritual

It is the High Priest/Priestess' duty to stand Ritual, presiding over the main body of that Ritual. He/she may, at their discretion, choose to have another person call the quarters and cast the Circle as well as perform certain duties during the Ritual. As the spiritual leader in Ritual, it is also their duty to see that anyone assigned duties during the Ritual is properly prepared and to oversee all aspects of the preparation. Ample time should be given to allow everyone the opportunity to learn their role in the Ritual, there is nothing more distracting than seeing someone reading from a script during Ritual. The HP/HPs may assign someone the task of ensuring everyone is well prepared for their part in the Ritual; however, ultimately they are responsible for the overall success.

The Attendees' Role in Ritual

This is an area often overlooked. Prior to leading the attendees into the Circle, they should be admonished as to the seriousness of Ritual (many do not know, have not been taught or have never attended a Ritual). They should be informed that speaking during the Ritual is unacceptable with the exception of responsive statements. Leaving the Circle (except for an emergency) without being "cut out" by a designee of the HP/HPs will damage the Circle's integrity and allow for negative energy to enter the space. If an attendee must leave the Circle, they should understand that they will not be allowed to re-enter because of the potential for admitting negative energy.

Phase 7: Earth Consciousness

All is connected... no one thing can change by itself.
Paul Hawken

In our modern society, man destroys the environment at such an accelerated rate that nature is incapable of keeping up. Before man, nature could readily and easily maintain the many ecosystems on the planet. She did this through the use of many techniques, drought, flood and fire (we have used irrigation as a tool for a very long time). These things allowed each ecosystem to remain intact and provide the necessary environment for the interrelated species of plants and animals that thrived in each.

As man progressed and the population expanded, much of the environment was damaged or destroyed to make room for more people. We brought in plants that were not native to the various areas in an effort to make our surroundings more pleasing. By doing this, we inadvertently changed the landscape and the ecosystems as well. Nature requires a delicate balance to allow the many plants and animals to live comfortably and the intro-duction of many non-native plants and animals has caused the native species to decline. Many non-native plants grow very aggressively and deplete the nutrients in the soil, which causes the native plants to starve. As the native plants die off, this causes the ecosystem to change and become inhospitable to native animals, which also starve. The introduction of non-native animals has much the same effect.

A good example would be that of the sand hill environment. We are not talking about a desert climate, far from it. This ecosystem is the natural habitat for a wide variety of plants and animals, many of which are now on the threatened or endan-gered list due to the destruction of the sand hills. Within this delicate environment you will find animals like the protected gopher tortoise, the fox squirrel, kestrels and others. Long leaf pine trees grow into beautiful giants; various grasses like the wire grass flourish. Many of these things could be potentially lost forever as this system declines from human encroachment and development. A large number of the native species of plants in this particular ecosystem are fire dependant, which means they require occasional fire to grow and flourish and to propagate. This was, in the past, the job of nature; handled by natural occurrences such as lightning strikes. But, because man has introduced so many invasive plants, much of the natives cannot grow to a height that will create these lightning strikes (these taller trees act as natural lightning rods).

Man has begun to learn the need to assist nature by using prescribed burns. Prescribed burns are very precisely planned operations that are carried out by teams trained in fire planning, ignition and control (and legally can only be done by those trained and certified in this area). The goal of these fires is to burn off the understory which contains the encroaching invasive plants as well as creating an environment for certain seeds to be able to germinate. They are planned using calculations involving wind, moisture and material. This is done to maintain a low moving fire which will not do damage to indigenous plants. This technique imitates what nature would eventually do, but on a more accelerated level. These burns rarely affect the native wildlife negatively, but actually serve to provide them increased access to natural food and shelter sources. These burns also stop the encroachment of plants in one habitat from crossing through the ecotone (this is for lack of a better description, the dividing line between environmental habitats). In many instances after a burn, teams re-enter the area and plant saplings and seeds of native species in an attempt to strengthen the zone. This is just one example of what many States are doing to ensure the survival of the many habitats found on this planet.

We have become a culture that seems to be blind to the

damage we do even at the smallest level. People routinely throw trash on the ground or out of their car window, even though every State has enacted laws against this (these laws are rarely enforced, further demonstrating that we have forgotten the damage it can do). Most of the products produced today take a very long time to decompose and in some instances become great hazards for the animals we share our world with.

Here is a list of how long it takes for some of our more common litter to decompose (obtained from **www.greenecoser vices.com/how-long-does-it-take-for-trash-to-biodegrade**):

Life Span of Litter

Aluminum Can: 200-500 years
Batteries: 100 years
Cardboard Box: 4 weeks
Cigarette Butt: Up to 10 years
Cotton Rag: 1-5 months
Disposable Diapers: 500-600 years
Glass Bottle: 1 million years
Leather: Up to 50 years
Lumber: 10-15 years
Monofilament Fishing Line: 800 years
Milk Cartons (plastic coated): 5 years
Nylon Fabric: 30-40 years
Orange Peel: 2-5 weeks
Paper: 2-5 months
Plastic Film Container: 20-30 years
Painted Wooden Stake: 13 years
Plastic 6-Pack Cover: 450 years
Plastic Bag: Up to 500 years
Plastic Coated Paper: 5 years
Plastic Soda Bottles: Forever
Rope: 3-14 months
Rubber Boot Sole: 50-80 years

Sanitary Pads: 500-800 years
Styrofoam: More than 5,000 years
Tin Cans: 50-100 years
Tin Foil: It does not biodegrade
Wool Clothing: 1-5 years

As you can see, these things do not just go away, in fact, most of them not only affect the appearance of our world, they become very hazardous to our wildlife. Litter kills or injures animals. Many small animals crawl into bottles or jars and get stuck and slowly starve to death. Animals get caught in plastic six-pack rings, plastic bags, fishing line and a multitude of throwaways. Birds that are stuck, can't fly away from danger. Sometimes animals caught in six-pack rings are strangled as they grow too big for the opening. Animals get cut, infected and die. Every year, millions of birds, fish and animals die from litter.

As a responsible member of the Clergy in an Earth-Based tradition, it is actually a part of your duty to educate your members and the public about the dangers that simple litter poses. There are a number of things you can do to help educate the public, the following list was obtained from **www.greenecoservices.com/12-ways-you-can-prevent-litter.** These are simple things you and your membership can do to help clean up our environment and educate the public at the same time. Doing these things will also serve to demonstrate your compassion for all living things.

Twelve Ways That You Can Prevent Litter

1.   Set an example by not littering.
2.   Pick up one piece of litter every day.
3.   Every week, pick up all the litter in front of your house, including the street.
4.   Ask your neighbors to properly dispose of their trash. Show them the difference between a clean area and an

area spoiled by litter, and stress why it's important to put trash in proper containers.

5. Make sure that your trash cans have lids that can be securely attached. If you have curbside trash service, don't put out unopened containers or boxes filled with trash.

6. Carry a litter bag in your car. Ask local businesses to buy car litter bags and distribute them to customers. Encourage them to print their names and an environmental message on the bag.

7. Ask your neighbors and or friends to join you in cleaning up one public area where litter has accumulated.

8. If you or a member of your family is involved in a civic group, scouting, or recreational sports program, encourage the group to become involved in a cleanup. Or have the group "adopt" a spot and maintain it on a regular basis.

9. Find out how you can plant and maintain flowers along a curb or sidewalk. People litter less where areas have been beautified.

10. Ask business owners to check their dumpsters every day to make sure tops and side doors are closed. If the business has a loading dock, ask them to keep it clean, and to put out a receptacle for employees to use.

11. Ask business owners to provide trash cans in front of their business with a sign: "Please do not litter".

12. If you own a construction or hauling business, make sure your trucks are covered when transporting material to and from sites. Use snow fencing around construction or demolition sites to prevent debris from being blown into other areas. Put trash containers on every floor for construction workers.

Pretty simple stuff, isn't it? Now imagine if everyone were to practice the things on this list, the United States currently has a population of about 315,763,542 and adds a new person about every 14 seconds (info obtained from **www.census.gov/ popclock**). Our landscape could be pristine. We know that we cannot get every single person to participate, but action tends to breed cooperation and involvement, give it a try. If you go out and start picking up a little trash in your community, I bet others will start doing a little bit too.

Participation in events such as Earth Day and Arbor Day can have a profound impact, not only on the community, but on our environment as well. The simple act of planting a single tree will reap many benefits through its life. Based on a research conducted by Professor T.M. Das of the University of Calcutta in India, a mature tree can raise a value of $193,250, and a tree living for at least 50 years generates $31,250 worth of oxygen, provides $62,000 worth of air pollution control, increases soil fertility to the tune of $31,250, recycles $31,250 worth of water, provides animal shelters worth $37,250, and prevents soil erosion, which is priceless. Das added that the figures earlier mentioned do not include the value of fruits, lumber or aesthetic beauty derived from trees, which, according to the Indian professor, is just an added sensible reason to take good care of forest resources (info obtained from **www.zoominfo.com /p/T.M.-Das/305343969**).

Actions in our daily lives add to the Green House Gases that enter our atmosphere. Until recently, no one considered that an issue, but it has been discovered that adding to these gases is helping to change our climate and not for the better. We can lower our impact quite easily if we just take the time to educate ourselves and others about the effects these gases have on our environment. Things as simple as what we buy, what we throw away, our travels and even choices we make in our homes all affect how much we each add to the problem.

There is an excellent online carbon footprint calculator

available free for use at **www.nature.org/greenliving/carboncal-culator**. It asks a series of questions and you simply check the boxes that apply. It will compare your footprint with the national average and this will help you adjust your lifestyle to have a more positive impact on our environment. By lowering the amount of Green House Gases we produce as individuals, we are creating a positive impact on our environment as a whole.

Green House Gases, when in the proper percentages, provide an important service; they help to regulate temperature and humidity. They do this by trapping a certain amount of infra-red heat and keeping it in our atmosphere. These gases have been on a steady rise since the beginning of the industrial revolution and are currently at a level higher than any point in the last 650,000 years. We contribute to this build up through the production of a number of chemical gases. Carbon dioxide, which is produced through the use of fossil fuels, contributes about 75% of the man made gases. Methane, which is a byproduct of the decomposition of waste in landfills and fossil fuel extraction, contributes about 14%. Nitrous oxide, which is produced by chemical fertilizers and many industrial processes, amounts to an additional 8% (Nitrous oxide is far more potent per gram than methane). Finally, we have fluorinated gases (more commonly known as CFCs) which are even more potent than nitrous oxide at 1%.

The burning of fossil fuels, such as coal and gasoline, contributes about over twenty seven billion tons of carbon dioxide in one year. The destruction of trees has had an amazing impact on our environment as well. Trees absorb a great deal of carbon dioxide. With trees being removed for expansion, we have a far smaller buffering agent to assist with the elimination of these gases; this allows the gases to remain in our atmosphere, which in turn elevates both the temperature and the level of humidity.

The way global warming will affect our weather/climate will be different from region to region. Places near the equator won't see large changes in temperature, but one thing that is sure is that places like the Arctic Ocean and Antarctica will become a lot warmer than normal. This will end up melting enormous quantities of ice and cause world ocean levels to rise, creating flooding in many coastal areas (about 60% of the world's population lives not far from a shoreline).

Everything we do, every choice we make, has a deep impact on our environment and on our quality of life. By doing nothing, you become part of the problem. Inaction still constitutes an action, although it becomes a negative one. We have been provided with many gifts, all the gifts we need to survive as a species and all that is needed to maintain all the life found in this world; be it man, animal or plant. It is up to us to recognize these gifts and become responsible stewards. Take the time to reach out and help maintain our world, take the time to educate others to the needs of the Earth Mother.

Permaculture

A practice which is receiving a great deal of attention lately is Permaculture. This is a sustainable living practice that is designed around three active rules, care for the Earth, care for the people and share the surplus.

It involves developing daily practice which allows you to create more than you use. This may sound a bit unrealistic given our modern lifestyle, but it can be achieved through conscious effort and planning. You should know that Permaculture does involve work and is not necessarily easy, but the outcome can be more than worth the effort.

The goals of Permaculture are to marry our modern lifestyle with the basic flow of nature. It involves adapting yourself to where you live and not adapting where you live to you. Earlier, we spoke of lowering your "carbon footprint". While that practice does indeed lower our destructive effect on our world, it does not replenish. Permaculture is a regenerative and sustainable practice that allows us to give back to the earth using many different methods. One of the most simple and effective is composting. This involves using the parts of the plants we grow, but do not use, to create fertilizer allowing us to perpetuate the growth process. Our planet has been doing this for millennia, but it is beginning to become a practice many are using to minimize our use of chemical fertilizers and therefore lower the damage we cause while improving the condition of our world.

These practices extend into all aspects of our daily lives including the design of homes that can filter water, diminish our reliance on fossil fuel heat and allow us to create and store electricity, once again lowering our impact and developing a surplus yield.

Much of this practice relies on observance, or biomimicry, to function. Modern science uses this in developing a number of things. By observing how nature handles things, we can develop methods of our own which will lower our impact on the global condition and in fact create an environment that will enrich both our lives and the condition of the Earth. There is a great deal of information on this subject and we touch on it here very lightly just to give you another idea for greening up your life and demonstrating our devotion to the Divine.

Incorporating some of the myriad environmentally conscious techniques will aid you in demonstrating the value of your chosen path and may create a doorway to further cooperation and understanding and this is truly what is important.

Phase 8: General Information

Alphabets

Theban Script

This alphabet, also known as the Witches Rune or the Runes of Honorius, was used in old times to transmit messages and store information safely as it was unreadable by those persecuting "Witches".

Ч-A ҷ-B ᴡ-C ᴔ-D ᴖ-E ᴡʏ-F ᴡʃ-G ᴕ-H ʋ-I ʋ-J ᴔ-K ᵧ-L
ᶾ-M ᴕₕ-N ᴔ-O ᴔ-P ᶾ-Q ᴔ-R ᵧ-S ᴢ-T ᴘ-U ᴘ-V ᴘ-W ᴕᵐ-X
ᴣ-Y ᴔₗ-Z

You have probably noticed some repetition of characters, this is because it is based on the old Latin alphabet (used during the time of Honorius, the mage who created it), which did not contain the letters J, U and W as found in our modern alphabet. The script is based on a single case structure; this has caused it to be determined as cipher language structure by many scholars.

Elder Futhark

It is unknown who first created this alphabet, but it is most likely of Germanic origin. Containing twenty-four symbols that correspond, phonetically, with a letter of the alphabet, each is associated with both a sound and a symbolic item or action. For simplification, the table is presented in reference to our current alphabet. Following that, they are shown in their proper order, with their general meanings:

ᚠ   A, Ansuz (God, Divinity)
ᛒ   B, Berkano (Birch, Twigs of Birch)
ᛗ   D, Dagaz (Day)

ᛗ   E, Ehwaz (Horse)

ᚠ   F, Fehu (Cattle, Riches, Property)

ᚷ   G, Gebo (Gift)

ᚺ   H, Hagalaz (Hail)

ᛁ   I, Isa (Ice)

ᛡ   J, Jera (Year, Harvest, Produce)

ᚲ   K, Kenaz (Boil, Carbuncle)

ᚱ   L, Laguz (Water) m-M, Mannaz (Man, Husband, Human Being)

ᛧ   N, Nauthiz (Suffer, Want, Crowd, Slavery)

ᛟ   O, Othala (Allodium, Land Holding, Inheritance)

ᛈ   P, Perthro (possibly Rock, Stone)

ᚱ   R, Raidho (Riding, Travel)

ᛋ   S, Sowilo (Sun, Power of the Sun)

ᛏ   T, Tiwaz (Warrior, the God Tyr)

ᚢ   U, Uruz (Primitive Ox, Wild Ox)

ᚹ   W, Wunjo (Good Fortune, Delight)

ᛉ   Z, Algiz (Elk)

ᚦ   TH, Thurisaz (Thorn, Giant, Troll)

ᛇ   EI, Eihwaz (Tree, Yew)

ᛜ   NG, Ingwaz (Phallus, Name of God)

Below, the runes are shown in their actual order:

ᚠ ᚢ ᚦ ᚨ ᚱ ᚲ ᚷ ᚹ ᚺ ᛧ ᛁ ᛡ ᛇ ᛈ ᛉ ᛋ ᛏ ᛒ ᛗ ᛖ ᛚ ᛜ ᛟ ᛞ

This runic alphabet served not only as a means of communication, but also as a divinatory tool. Standing Stones can be found across the European Continent that are engraved with these icons, some of the stones date back to approximately 100 BCE.

Over the course of the past seventy-five to one hundred years, some traditions have developed their own alphabet for use inside of their belief system. We have chosen to only include those of a historical nature pre-dating modern, so-called Neo-Pagan systems. This is not done to invalidate any system's methods, but to focus on the older more well known documentation.

Wheel of the Year

The Wheel of the Year contains the eight primary holy days of the Pagan/Earth-Based path. While there are a number of lesser celebratory days within our culture these eight are considered to be high holy days. Following both solar and lunar movement as well as agricultural events, these days have held immense meaning and value throughout the Pagan community for many centuries.

Being an Earth-Based system, great emphasis was placed on the movement of the Sun and Moon as well as harvest and planting. These events portray the cycle of life and were exceed-ingly important in a time when calendars and clocks were unavailable.

Quarters

The Quarter Days of the Wheel are aligned with the Solstices and Equinox, or changing of the seasons and are considered to be the lesser Sabbats. When set to the commonly used Gregorian calendar they are as follows:

1st Quarter day (Spring or Vernal Equinox). This falls between March 19th and 21st and is associated with Ostara.

2nd Quarter day (Summer Solstice). Falls between June 20th and 22nd known as Litha.

3rd Quarter day (Fall or Autumnal Equinox) known as Mabon.

4th Quarter day (Winter Solstice). Falls between December 20th and 23rd and is known as Yule.

Cross Quarter Days

The Cross Quarters are generally aligned with Lunar movement and are associated with planting and harvest times.

1st Cross Quarter day falls on February 2nd and is known as Imbolc.

2nd Cross Quarter day falls on April 30th and is known as Beltane.

3rd Cross Quarter day falls on August 1st and is called Lugnasadh

4th Cross Quarter day falls on November 1st (usually celebrated on Oct. 31st,) and is called Samhain.

The use of the Wheel of the Year serves to emphasize our connection to the Earth and all of nature. It demonstrates the values and importance of the cycle of life that we are all a part of and it helps us to remember that connection and maintain reverence to the Divine.

Final Words

You still have far to go in your journey. The Second Degree has taught you much, but there is still much ahead. Continue on, for even after the Third Degree your spiritual journey will still have only just begun. Blessings.

Moon Books invites you to begin or deepen your encounter with
Paganism, in all its rich, creative, flourishing forms.